Thigh HIGHS and NO LIES

Memoir by:
Being_Brooklin

BROOKLIN BOWDLER WEIDERMAN

Copyright © 2023 Brooklin Bowdler Weiderman
All rights reserved
First Edition

Fulton Books
Meadville, PA

Published by Fulton Books 2023

ISBN 979-8-88982-172-4 (paperback)
ISBN 979-8-88982-173-1 (digital)

Printed in the United States of America

"The many lives I survived, stayed alive,
determined to overcome, to now serve."
Brookie

"Full names vary to protect those I love"

Preface

**Trauma is an illusion
This isn't our fault or for us to hold on to.
That is the illusion**

Pretty sure we can all agree that failure is a part of life. It's painful. Experiencing downs is knowing what it means to get up. In that I have learned to reshape failure.

However, this book isn't about getting back up because we make jackass moves or bad choices. This is about how we get back up, why we get back, if we get back up.

This story is about overcoming significant trauma and still being able to achieve your dreams.

We have two choices: We get up and fight or take flight. How we feel after trauma is mostly the same.

Mostly, we feel disgusting, sad, and bad.
Regardless.
We fight for ourselves.
Ignore the naysayers
Most in our heads
Ignore what others say.
This is our journey.
It's our fight.

I'm so sorry you were hurt.

I'm sorry if no one chose to believe you. I am here typing aimless, some seemingly poetic thoughts on this subject. However, stick around.

You decide, you're in charge. You're not hopeless.

Yet, still reliving my past alone had me feeling like I was drowning my brain, as it seeped into my mind. Where your thoughts are formed and your memories can unwind. The articulation of the pain has begun, no it's not fun. But it has to mutha fuckin' be done to put it blunt. My brain tried to drown my pain, compartmentalizing my hurt, even referring to me with disdain.

I wanted love. Though strong, I knew and believed what happened to me when I was a child was wrong.

There are many ways to heal. Feeling, therapy, and my next book on accidental manifestation.

Think about your future and who you know you WILL BE!

Do you relate?

Finally, in my late twenties, I began to see.

I thought my mind was fucking with me. Our brain plays hide-and-seek with the trauma that exists.

No matter how old you are, the truth exists forever. I wish I could promise you it all goes away after you begin your journey of truth.

I can tell you this.

Since healing began, I exist in the here and now, as opposed to swatting away memories that crept into my mind—coming from the back of my brain, again and again.

The conscious mind and brain are very different spaces. Why I've mentioned them, sounding ridiculous, by omission. Our brain holds onto the dirty, dusty memories, keeping them far away from our conscious mind.

Trauma is like a train heading our way.

The ticket somehow already paid. That doesn't mean you have to jump on this fast tracked train. My story isn't about dodging the train. I got right on it. Choosing that way only carries us to more painful choices.

You don't have to board the runaway train. But, feelings lead to healing. For some reason, having feelings is still taboo, even today.

We have to feel to heal.

Question: Does that sound simple to you?

People say, they say it like it is. It is, however, crucial.

Yet most of us still run in circles. This train speeds up every time we make another poor choice.

It's not because we're incapable of making the right choices, as is the case according to society. It's simply because we weren't taught.

We had to hide the lies after we were hurt. Many of us were left without anyone. Not allowed to talk openly.

Whether our innocence was stolen by a person, place, or thing. There are so many traumas that are done to us, and we carry the shame.

Why was it time to tell you mine?

I don't know why my heart was finally ready after years of being asked to tell my story. Fear, insecurities, I mean I can't count the ways I was kept from sharing. I was even flat-out lazy.

Then finally, at forty, after six years of jumping off my train of hell, so much had changed. I jumped off to feel, I was battered and bruised when I rolled through the mud I landed in. It wasn't pretty. Nor was it an easy decision to jump off.

It wasn't easy to say stop my abuser as a child either. And still that day my *no* was taken away. Writing a book is scary if you worry about what others will think. What was more important to me was all that is lost for children due to being abused and traumatized. It became a burden I could no longer carry anymore.

The fact that, still, decades later, there is such suffering is absolutely surreal. My story is my own, and so is yours.

Reading every detail of that night like a book, my memories of my past good and evil are still vivid—even as my toddler is needing a snack, and I am needing to type. I have to break and come back.

Life will always tell you it's too busy. And it seems so, yet, you can accomplish anything you want.

This book, however, has been mostly finished for two weeks. But the moment I was about to send in my last manuscript or—the collection of my life—to my publishers, more revealed itself.

I have to stop adding, so I can get to you.

This is only the first book. So…

Here we go.

***

Unfortunately, even the person you think you trust the most may be the person who walks in, passes by, even seeing exactly what is happening. Here's what I'm trying to convey. The trauma has only just begun for the victim. However, you're weeping isn't heard or seen through their eyes wide open. Rather, their shut eyes. The only way I can say it kindly today is she froze from shock and chose not to feel anything. In my story, I'm vividly honest.

Today, I can say she must have freeze-framed my pain and chosen to walk away. She somehow let it fade—leaving me with all the shameful pain and unanswered questions.

Therapists have told me over and over again, even a simple hug at ten after my life-changing traumatizing event was enough to change my future. A hug isn't so simple at all. Now there are hug therapy retreats because of the importance of a hug. A hug could've changed my life almost completely. I wouldn't have made many of my poor choices from anger, loneliness, and ignorance. So you can imagine the blame shifting from my abuser to who walked in and didn't help me.

However, the choice to be angry and unkind based on your own confusion and unhealed pain isn't any way to live either.

That is part of my hope in telling you my story. Many may think my typing up my emoir, based on reality with some vivid recollections about life after trauma at forty is only something an egomaniac would achieve. Nothing could be further from the truth. Now we should be hoping to open Pandora's box. Am I her? Y'all I don't know, this has been a full labor of love. This has been healing, but in a way I never expected. Losing so many people for telling the truth of my traumas, that it is still on the news today.

You think this is the label I ever wanted. Jesus, No.

This is the hardest thing I have ever done.

It's been a process of purging so much of what was my shield, yet keeping me down. My soul felt baron, yet with so much fruit and love to give. I had to get past the life chosen for me before I was born, overcome the shame. Let go of the blame.

I can no longer live a life that doesn't align with mine. I hope reading this book will bring you out of the dark, from under the covers, or even the crossroads that lead you here.

Many would rather let secrets lie, well I tried, however, it is almost monthly now a huge story breaks about a nine through twelve year old girl raped by someone trusted, related, wore not protected or believed. These same girls may not make it later in life.

Like most, nobody took the fucking chance to have the big R talk with me. It is scarlet in memory. Not everyone will be able to compartmentalize, be so bold as to believe there is a good God who has his ways to make everything we endure into something someone else won't have to, (at all) is a stretch, but knowledge and courage is power. So is compassion for all those who need my memory bank to hopefully help access their pain.

Tapping into this book may not work for everyone, matter of fact, if I tapped into every book I opened, well shit I wouldn't be able to get anything done, including my destiny. So I don't take it personally.

Everything and anything takes courage and faith. My way of writing is a place you have never been, and that is scary for me. I take you to the hardest places in my life. The movements and moments I share are vivid and real, since I was raped.

There I said it. And worse even still, I was only ten. Worse even still, it is *still* happening every few minutes across the world and possibly right next door.

What is the first steal to face the truth?

1) Beware of triggers.
2) Knowing healing is coming.
3) Choosing to journal and share with a professional.

Facing the truth in essence.

This book is like rolling thunder with scattered storms. It's about continually getting up as much as I've fallen.

The abuse of children is an epidemic that leads to only more heartache and brokenness, causing most of today's statistics. I became every single thing the world deems wrong.

It is time for the world to think the opposite. It has long been, "They need to get it together." No more. Instead, it's finally time to take a compassionate stance. It's time to ask the real question and accept the reality you may hear and the tears you may feel.

What everyone should be asking compassionately is, "What really happened to them?"

I'm guilty of my many transgressions and much wasted time. The worst is hurting so many people I loved—while asking myself, "Why am I this way?" It wasn't until I was in my thirties that I really began to call this memory by name and demand it to stop hiding from me.

As a trauma counselor, I see myself in the faces staring back at me—all in different stages of their own healing. I am always asked, "How long until it doesn't hurt?" I don't have an exact timeline for you. I do have the same answer, always affirming their courage in starting this process at all. Watching them grow and see that life isn't about blame or aiming your pain at anyone in the way is truly amazing.

It's a new surreal.

Thigh Highs and No Lies

I sit and reflect daily, often alone staring at nothing in particular yet lost in thoughts of the moments I myself missed. I especially overanalyze all discord in my life to this day. Some damage can't be undone. We can't expect everyone to understand, some don't even believe in abuse. That needs to change, it only causes more abuse. But when we become whole and change into a strong, honest, and hardworking human being—no longer the damsel in distress or a woman who is more of a little girl than we were before we started healing.

I wonder what I've done for someone to suddenly choose hate versus love and respect. Then I remind myself, many don't face their own trauma. Why would they care of mine? Even when it begins to fall off me piece by piece?

Trauma recognizes trauma. The company you keep will not be the same, for the most part, after you open your heart—especially, when your lips part more with laughter. You are new, bright, and no longer blue, to make it rhythm for you. It is true that you will lose more and more people the better you get. However, you will gain more as you grow. There will be those who stay even if they don't quite understand the new you? They'll recognize the fallen pieces of you, following you into the new life speaking out has made you to be stronger. Sadly, even decades-long relationships full of a history of being open with one another may suddenly stop, as they get off the train we've been on. You may feel left behind in spite of it all. Trauma bonds are as strong as any other love.

Don't get stuck back there, like I have a thousand times before. Why? I couldn't let go of someone I loved—even though they may have been done trying to love me. Too many questions? How could you leave me now? I thought you loved me? You may know that childish scenario. Breakups are hard, no matter why.

What I can say is this: Believe in yourself, your journey, and where it is leading you. Don't wait until forty to finally be free. This could have happened years ago. Timing is everything. I have stopped being angry at the wasted years with him, him, this and that, because now I have absolute closure and will never look back.

Trust yourself and your mind when it shows you pieces of the puzzle you have been searching for without even knowing it. I can now say, I became a stranger by choice. I wasn't left or thrown away.

I am not awful, as they will say out of their own misunderstood pain.

It comes from their *trauma*. There's that word. It annoys many. Trust me, I'm aware.

Today I can think with clarity. It isn't you or me. They just don't see what I see, and that's OK. Change is scary. The brighter your light, the dimmer others may feel. What is it? Freedom.

It's neither your intention nor your problem to solve. You can't make anyone understand or care if they suddenly don't recognize you. Your inner self is glowing brightly. Watching you be so kind almost grosses them out. They won't let you change. They want you to fight like you used to.

One day soon, you will stop the same back-and-forth routine. How could you not fight for everything when you were overtaken by someone you trusted, or you lost someone without warning, especially young? How could you not think everything was against you if you were diagnosed with cancer at a young age, like one of my children. When you're forced to fight for your life only days after a dance recital? Not knowing days later you would never be the same. Trauma looks different even if it is the same type, such as sexual abuse. However, it has the same lasting effects on us no matter who or what stole your chance to grow as you would have without such sudden and unnatural breaches in life.

Beauty is not being perfect. I am adding this the day before I send this book to my publisher. I have been typing for nine and a half months. It's time to give birth. *But* today I learned something about myself.

Think of those people, places, or things we still hold on to. I realized there was a question: How am I writing this book, a therapist no more, and still living part of my former double life?

How was I going to publish this book without telling you how healing changes so rapidly once you begin? How could I do so with-

Thigh Highs and No Lies

out telling you the painful parts that could also be happening as your life looks different and so do you?

I am sharing a lot early, because the sooner you get well, deep down—having time to reach inside and pull out the roots—the better. When I had open wounds that were so close to being sewn up, my own family would seem to fall apart around me and leave me there only half-healed. I would find myself screaming, "You won't let me change. You all want me to be sick and quiet."

A child should never be exposed to such enduring pain. Holding onto secrets out of fear causes impulsive behaviors and outbursts that feel uncontrollable—as well as the many addictions that tend to follow. These are all coping mechanisms adding to the trauma receptors in our brain. They dull our ability to care for ourselves and, worse, others outside our own unacknowledged pain.

Our need to express the truth is also about taming the lion inside—the one that claws away and causes us to react in ways we don't want to. This is probably one of the truest statements I've known and experienced myself from both sides.

I seem too forgiving to many. However, I have only grace to give—after so many selfish years pacifying myself because I knew no other way, only to come home well after treatment, with my strong views and determination to achieve so many missed opportunities. I want you to know that many will back away, unsure how to be unhealthy around the new healthier you.

Eventually the lies will be deep as we grow shallow in our thoughts. If we go too deep, we see it.

Worse, my children, decades later, would be hurt by my overgrown insecurities from buried pain. Life isn't all dark or light. You have every right to find out why you feel the way you do. Asking what happened is incredibly important. Today, the resources online and the ability to call anonymously is a start in society. Abuse of any kind is trauma. When your *no* is taken away is my definition of trauma.

Trauma causes shame.
Shame is an illusion.

What will change this is believing a victim, so they can become a survivor.

It's personal collusion (terrorism to the soul). If we could stop the trauma, wouldn't that be surreal? However, the facts of life are inevitable, good and evil. We are walking on a moving sphere with billions of other humans. We don't know what they're thinking or, worse, what they aren't.

If I could make sure you hear one thing, it would be without a doubt, *It wasn't your fault.*

The sadness, though, at times will be unbearable. This is the only direct road to healing. If we heal the first time, we can avoid piling on more pain. Doing so covers up the original root. It grows and eventually makes it almost impossible to recognize yourself underneath the rooted tree of growing pain inside you.

Even after so much work on myself through therapy, I still have messy hours of talking to a friend and overanalyzing. Why? I've had a broken heart even recently. All things come to some sort of an end. Even the obvious can be difficult; watching my children grow so fast has been devastating at times.

Since I have accomplished dreams while healthy, I have lost a handful of "close" friends. All have been in the industry, and all, the most surprising ones to find walking away.

I craved being whole and healthy most of my life but was held back by loving the wrong people. I knew it was possible deep down before Ted Talks and Dr. Google and my own education told me. I had to learn not to ask why. This is another thing I would recommend. Don't ask why—if you can.

The only real answers around being traumatized are they were mentally ill. Being in the wrong place at the wrong time is another main cause of anything traumatizing.

In my case, my abuser had been around me many times. And though there were moments I was deeply uncomfortable around him as young as four, it wasn't until I was ten that the next chapter and the true beginning of this horrific event took place—stealing everything from me in those short fifteen minutes.

Thigh Highs and No Lies

I heard the clock tick, saw the sun begin its descent behind where I was taken and the floodlights blinding me, causing him to stumble. Though my hair was already stuck to my tear-soaked face, still I saw the terror in his eyes. I already knew it was wrong. But in that moment, something hit me deeply. Many who suffer from sexual trauma of any type will then internalize the frightening feelings we feel. Energy spreads faster than anything in this world, the same as the energy between humans. The fastest spreading energy is negative. Positivity, if consistent, is contagious.

But for some reason, true joy and happiness are fleeting. On the other hand, we will dwell on so many things for hours, days, and weeks. And many will become fully depressed as a result of not having the tools to bounce back.

I will be sharing with you my deepest pains, my greatest joys, my worst heartbreaks, and what contentment means today. This is where I begin. And now, it's the day before I turn you in—my book, all these pieces of me. I added more to a simple poem because my spirit opened up even more. I did so not to bore or overshare; I work hard at not repeating myself, unless absolutely necessary. The things I do repeat are the very things that truly made years of agony become less and less agonizing with time as I healed. Also, my understanding that others' actions have little to do with my growth.

Reliving half of this book has brought me to my knees, cradling the inner child in me. I've heard recent "former friends'" horrible threats and name-calling. They only wanted to hurt me enough not to write this book or so I wouldn't feel good enough to do the *Maxim* magazine cover shoot next month.

These were the same phrases I heard from my own mother for years.

It's just confirmation that the devil walks this earth, and he is terrified of the light being shined on the pain of children and adults everywhere. I still believe in loyalty. No one will take that strength away from me. Hate and cruelty is a choice I will never make. And if I slip in the moment, I am never above asking for forgiveness immediately.

A big victory in life will be when you realize people's twisted, inhumane behavior has very little to do with you.

It's not that I'm special for taking on life and the facts. We are strong and brave. Hear that.

I want to spread as much fearlessness and ways of moving forward after pain as I could. There will be many in your life who will choose to go, rather than stay. It's the rules of gravity. We are pulled apart for our lives to turn out the right way. You could hope for it all. And maybe one day you will have it.

I only say maybe, as it never looks like what you thought it would. Us humans are always making plans, as God laughs while he makes himself known.

Somehow, others can make us forget how hard we fought—how we always get up. Get up before the train takes over your life.

Regardless of when you jump off or feel numb, you didn't fail. You are brave and will start to feel. Welcome to the land of the living. It took me until I was thirty-three years old to open the invitation to life, no questions asked. I threw my dope down the drain and spent eleven days in detox sick—with my family not even wanting me home.

However, when your heart turns for real, those who are supposed to be there will be, and they will never hurt you. None of it's our fault, and we're alive to tell. Abuse is trauma causing shame.

Shame is an illusion,

Collusion

Telling us it's our fault.

Tells us we aren't enough

And how love must be bought.

Everything earned.

Telling you you're *fucked*!

Until we turn a corner and see for ourselves. In the dawn of light, we realize we aren't the ones who bite. We were bitten with hate and pain, disillusioned by the shame that is an illusion.

CHAPTER 1

No Sugar Coating It

The night my "NO" was taken away, I knew then what true agony was. Then confusion and of course anger. I lost my first battle with the devil himself that evening. I thought I was defeated for thirty-three years. It would be that long before I'd learn that we don't lose if we get up, no matter what we look like when we do. We could be bloody, weeping, or mad as fuck, just as long as we get up.

And I did get up. But I didn't realize, for decades, what I'd survived. I played the victim, not knowing any other way. I was stuck back in time, back when I was raped and no one protected me. It was that unhealed pain that would keep me on the train of bad choices. And it was my healing that brought this book out of me.

If only I'd had a safe person to talk to. Even a hug from my mother—who had walked into my horror the moment I screeched from pain, though my cry was quickly silenced. But, it was too late. Not until I lost my virginity years later would it begin to register, it still not the word rape. Yet, I would never be the same. Worse, nothing was explained to me, ever.

He fumbled off me with unbuttoned pants. And my bikini bottoms were clearly on the floor, where they'd been kicked by me. I was woken abruptly and fought him when he removed them. Believing someone would surely save me, I fought. I had no idea my mother would be the only person I would never truly be able to trust again.

Instead, like an animal, I kicked. And though frantic, I gently asked why I wasn't in my bed. It's me. It's me.

He looked up, and I saw a man I had known most of my life. But his eyes were no longer the same; they were demonic. And he told me firmly, while touching me, "Shh, no one can hear you, and this will be quick. It may hurt, but I don't want to hurt you."

I just remember saying, "What? Why? Ouch, what are you doing?"

He told me to relax and that it would feel good.

He did things to me. Then there was a noise in the bathroom next door, and he rushed on top of me as I looked away. I was already done for; I was no longer there. I stared at the posters on the wall and into the floodlights shining so bright. The sun had gone down quickly I thought. How long was I here? Where was I?

I then started to raise my voice. "Stop! I can't breathe." I screamed as the pain split me in half. He was at least over six feet and a grown man. My screech was clearly heard by the person next door, who I knew was my mother. It was her stomach problems, Otherwise, she would never have come so far. There were at least three bathrooms between where he took me and the pool party. It could have been ten to fifteen minutes from when he picked my completely relaxed, sleeping body up.

I was all alone in the third den. I was jet-lagged and had fallen asleep while watching Nickelodeon with ten or so other kids. I was in an oversized T-shirt over a damp bikini when I was put into bed. I remember being picked up and asking for my mommy. And I agreed when he said, "You must be cold."

I was still half asleep, so I agreed and assumed he would get my mom. That was when it all changed, and instincts kicked in. Which was to kick and scream. But I had no voice. I was in a nightmare I couldn't wake up from. I began to cry, and he assured me that it was OK, and it was better or some shit. I would rather not say. But I was soon silently weeping. I felt so disgusted. That world still really hurts and triggers a deep pain in me to this day.

That night, I began to realize I was afraid. But my weeping made him want more. I went into shock as he did things and shot something on me. He then grabbed the blanket and wiped it off. He was breathing so hard, and I had no idea what had happened. I hoped it was over as I fixed my gaze between the window and the posters on the wall.

That's when he got on top of me, a tiny ten-year-old me who was traumatized and had no clue what had just happened. And he still had to hurry and shove himself inside me, knowing someone was next door. The pain shocked me, and I screeched. But let's skip the part of my mother not handling this or helping me at all. That "should" be a chapter of its own—called a "twilight zone."

Instead, let's get straight to the hours until dawn. I saw drops of blood. I figured it was mine, as he seemed to be fine. And I could barely walk. But I needed to get clean. I would have jumped in the shower immediately. But I was afraid by my mother's instructions and her annoyed yet assured voice. "Stay here, don't move, and be quiet."

I was back in a fetal position, hyperventilating by this point. I was told to dry it up and be quiet. "It couldn't be that bad?" She said. You just had a bad dream." She never questioned why I was half nude, why I was across the house from my room, or why I was so scared. To her, it was someone I should trust. And I was too afraid to tell her what he had done. Hair matted to my face, I didn't know what to call what had happened to me. How could I explain that this man, who I was supposed to trust, had just split me in half?

It wouldn't be until I chose to lose my virginity years later that I realized a grown man treated me like a fuck at ten. Then, when rushed, he still had to rape me, even after already being "relieved."

CHAPTER 2

My Choice

When I lost my virginity, which was a happy and beautiful moment, I was trying so hard not to think about or figure out what had truly happened to me. And many others are also hurt or confused when they are tricked into being told all the things I'd been told. Sadly, I was too disgusted to feel special. When I chose to make love, similar things were done to me. But this time, I wanted it. I even lifted my shirt when my boyfriend came.

The first signs of conditioned trauma were when I repeated the worst night of my life to make a man happy. What the hell? Now I knew what had happened to me as a child.

If you are confused about being molested, raped, or sexual deviance, it's normal for both sexes. Had it happened more than once, I shudder to think how much worse it would have become. This vivid memory ruined my life for decades. So if you're reading this, know that trauma isn't always violent, but it is always confusing. How did I know it was wrong? It was because of who it was, and I was still playing with dolls. Then there were all the secrets. I had just started having sleepovers away from home. I was a child.

So, do I delete the details and keep it simple? "I was abused by a person I knew. Just a handful of years later I felt safe and no longer a child. I felt him inside me and I wanted more. I wasn't afraid. Did it matter to "him", then yes it did.

We made love again, I screeched loudly, without realizing anything by this point. He looked shocked! I panted, "please don't stop." This moment I remember, heart to hear, trying to make it through this story to the best parts. Our climax changed my life. This was making love or love, or just sex? This question my trauma would mess with me for years. For the next few years I felt love and mostly I felt I was free.

I wasn't, follow me...

It was so beautiful and then I became afraid of a man who had taught me real love. I still become overwhelmed with anxiety when I have to go back there.

That night, when I finally climbed into bed, after crying fresh tears with less fear. Feeling stupid and raw too, he wanted me to put on my sheer black panties.

I didn't feel special or forever, I felt safe and the pleasure of him intoxicated me. know this, I was setting myself free.

There is a difference between us, it's not all the same or always except for one thing. Letting go of the past and judgment. Clearly making the best choices in a flash has caused so much extra.

But eventually, while writing this book I still don't notice the differences. All the same I thought?

I am moving home in a few weeks. Maybe there are new beginnings everywhere, with anyone who had love for the broken you.

CHAPTER 3

Demonic Eyes

For decades, I was told, "It wasn't that bad." Time passed, decades in fact.

I was told, "It was all in your head."

You can imagine where I spent the better part of thirty years and why I felt it was *all in my head*. Years ago when I was first asked to write a book, flashes of this moment zip-lined through my mind, as if I was just as naive now as I had been at ten. I wanted to tell my story, but I didn't know where to start. I tell my clients, just start, and the healing will come. So, here I am, too, with you. I had to put this into words. Writing is my only way of absolving the life I may have had *if*.

In life, the middle is *if* (let that sink in).

Only words of truth endure, and my truth may horrify you at times. Then other parts of my life were absolutely amazing and surreal, from the outside looking in especially. Words and our voices have power superior to us, as you never know who's listening or reading. *Timing* is another dirty word—once upon a time. I always felt that being in the wrong place at the wrong time seemed to be my destiny. I hope you don't dwell on that cliché. Life is well now. It has been ever since, I've finally gotten enough healing myself—over more years than ought to have passed.

I do know where we start.

As I'm typing, I constantly keep thinking, *What's relevant?* What I know for sure is that I thought I could handle shit—even back then, at just ten. It's the same today.

Now I know we are all still our inner children. We are still learning and unlearning what we were taught.

I was taught to dry it up and get over it—"it" being just about anything. My mother hated crying and certainly was never the kind of person I could talk to.

A sister was my main caretaker. Don't know her anymore. She isn't no longer who she was before and writing this book was part of my plan to never stop going, dreaming and never settling no matter how others treat you, never tell your dreams, just be friends. Even now at forty-one to her fifty-two, she is still set it. Never truly having a sister relationship, rather than a soke one sided rivalry is heartbreaking. We all have purpose and can't be afraid or trying to keep up with the Jones relationship is something we are working on. She was my saving grace for sure. Had she been there that summer, nothing would have happened to me. But she wasn't as she had to live her life too.

Wisdom is not just hearing knowledge. Wisdom is truth. It's experiencing life on life's terms. However, when it comes to your truth, no one can take that from you. It's a beautiful and humble character trait (truth).

I write the way I talk. As I type, I'm still blocking out his demonic eyes and my shock at who was doing this to me. That is the worst part; over 85 percent will know their abuser. I look back now and remember the entitlement he felt, the confidence in his words while hurting me in the worst way. He hurt me in all ways, emotionally and physically and broke my spirit as a growing girl who needed to believe in something. I lost hope in something greater. His actions broke my belief that anyone, much less God, cared about me.

However, God does care about you. And the truth, as they say, is "What doesn't kill you makes you stronger." It also makes us survivors. We are dangerous, with nothing to lose when we finally realize our secret and shame was never ours to bear.

Shame the illusion I keep articulating, as well as typing. But each time something had to be freed from me. First my long dark ponytail let loose, freed. But we I shook it and giggle I realized hair in my face I was alone making a weirdo out of myself. I ended up laughing out loud as I walked to the coffee bar at one of these artsy places I loved at home on the hill, but in the south, they bored me and no one's eccentricities inspired me. I will tell you what always did if I caught a hairs eye. Exeially when won't mess by those who torture me more than they know. Yet babies cooed and figured with me. Your smile and warmth and would dul eyee mommy mother's amazing grin shame said she is why breastfeeding and natural food became me, but what never became of her was the wrath of my mother. The only one left. Of course they choose just scoops over Atlanta and acted all sad, wje. God knows living near my mom is a one way tunnel and it only blows one way. He nonesens toward you. Most succumbz t's put on us by our abuser.

Read that as many times as you have to. When I told my psych professor my analogy, she added it to her curriculum. That was one of my true confirmations; I was destined to tell you about the night I was told to forget. It was this twilight evening. It wasn't quite dark when I was picked up and taken to the most desolate part of the house during a pool party in honor of our visit.

The incident was partly why psychology became so important to me. I couldn't figure out how anyone could stray from an otherwise healthy life. Their minds were not wired right. The man who hurt me was not immediate family and not always a disappointment. He was funny and attended church with his gorgeous, kind wife and daughters of his own.

This secret would ultimately be one still festering or forgotten. I'm opening Pandora's box, because too many are hurting. I see children, adults, and teens, to this day, fighting demons that aren't theirs to fight. They were transferred when their abusers couldn't hold them in themselves any longer.

Soul ties are real and can be broken by you alone—no magic, just boldness.

Mine was *rape*, a word I didn't associate with what happened to me for decades.

Where the pain truly began was when it no longer felt safe to be me. Where the fire in my belly had actually been lit, and my destiny prevailed from the worst moments of my life.

Thigh Highs and No Lies

What happened to me happened when I was still climbing cherry trees, charging the neighborhood kids for Jane Fonda-like aerobics classes. That—sigh—like many things in my life, ended abruptly.

I remember always having some smart-ass thing to say. I have much older siblings. Thus, I knew a lot more than kids in sandboxes. I had been pretty independent since around seven. Born a fighter, I wasn't easily afraid.

My mother shushing me if I uttered a whimper of the horror that rocked my world is hard for many to fathom. The secret would become hers, mine, and his.

It'd remain all the way to my seventh rehab, where I finally broke down. I couldn't take it anymore. All my relationships had been ruined as my increasing pain had grown like a tree with limbs inside my mind, body, and soul. I felt like a scarecrow.

I will tell you how the truth was forced out of me to the very moment. I was fuckimg thirty-three, so many years were wasted by fear and shame.

Hopefully, this book will be published by the time I'm forty-one, so many can finally be free of the flying saucers of visuals in our minds—captivating our entire existence. Yes, captivating; that's how we survive. The nightmares still plague me. We all want to be free ultimately, right?

I hope as you read these pieces of me, my life, the hope, the good, the great, the unthinkable, and the utter despair. Then back again to hope.

Even as I somehow explain when every day what was normal for others used to become obsessions for me—or the opposite; I wouldn't give a fuck. I've always been obsessed with helping others, even if it meant losing my own opportunities, even letting go of dreams. I don't regret choosing motherhood and dance over *Girl, Interrupted*. However, the universe always does it right. So what is my fulfillment, universe?

I focused on what strengths I knew I had. This gave me purpose in life. I'm talking about the dreams we daydream as a kid, while in math class, staring aimlessly out the window. Back then, even before

I was ten and the ultimate betrayal, my view was mountains. We lived in the Valley of Europe then. Luckily, I was good at compartmentalizing, and some of those daydreams did come true.

I still remember shivering and how it hurt to physically pull the heavy, white, floral, ugly early '90s duvet over me. I didn't dare moan. I couldn't stop weeping, though silently. For the first time, I can describe exactly what I saw—from the lioness in me, alive and present even then.

First, I was a young girl, a child.

I remember the physical pain, embarrassment, sheer terror. I was scared my privates would show if I stood up. My mother had barged in like she was there for me. She was only there because of a noise, my scream. After that, she wished she'd never seen what she saw.

I wanted to yell, "I'm ten. Then, I wondered, "Wait, am I still ten? I wanted to express the fact that I don't know why I was hurting down there. But I knew who had made me hurt. I remember suddenly thinking, *Oh my God. I'm not me anymore.* I instantly became deeply sad. That sadness would last for many years, off and on. But I fought my way through with dancing. By that time I had my first sexual relationship with an older boyfriend. This was my first statistic, as society says.

Only hours before I was raped, I had been playing Marco Polo, swimming with other kids on a hot summer. Then all I wanted was my mom to hold me and tell me I would be OK. After all, she had seen enough to know her child was hurt.

I quietly whimpered for the last time in my life, "Mommy?" She glared at me and was having trouble standing up. Was she in shock, too? I didn't know. I do know the rest of my sentence was spoken silently to myself, *Why won't she pick me up and hold me?* I kept thinking, *Why isn't she yelling at him or freaking out?* Then I realized, all I cared about was her scooping me up and crying with me. She didn't.

Instead, I was told, "Don't leave the room." I finally looked at her. Clearly, I was weeping and had been. She looked directly into my big, usually bright blue eyes, now bloodshot, and for a split second, I saw her shock, even pain, certainly fear. Was she unsure how to respond to me? How? As a mother now, I could never ever not hold my babies. And I can't promise you that, when the cops got there, the abuser would look the way he had when they got there. That is how I protect mine.

However, she firmly told me to be quiet. I nodded and turned my back, still covered in an ugly floral duvet—and in pain. I was left in a ball facing the wall. I could hear them whispering, which still puzzles me to this day. Then I was alone, me and that duvet. I was full of fear of what was underneath. I was in pain and felt a dampness between my legs. I heard him stumbling. I shivered, realizing I had little control over my body—not like I did before. I couldn't stop weeping, though still silently.

Have you felt so alone around someone who used to hold you just because and now they seemed to feel nothing when you needed it the most?

Friends, this is the worst rejection.

It paved the way for a life full of bad choices, especially making relationships with men so fucking confusing. One minute, I cared. And the next, I'd forget If I ever gave a fuck. Today there's a name for it—*ghosted*. Back then, in the '90s and 2000s, we just stopped calling or receiving calls. Before text began, relationships were much simpler. However, I do wish there were camera phones, recordings, and shit. Google even would have enabled me to look up what had happened to me.

I will be talking about life in Hollywood. It's bizarre. But first, I have to stop skipping around and tell you the absolute most perverted, stomach-curling moment in my life. It was my first brush with death (emotional death, that is).

You'd think accomplishing my larger-than-life dreams would make it all go away one day—or having money would cure my past. Nothing does, except truth, love, and acceptance.

Trauma is hard to face. It's like not knowing what to say when your friend loses a family member—even if you've been there and can imagine but go frozen.

Today there are resources for everything, and we care and believe every word you say. The beginning of healing is feeling heard.

Breathe. You aren't alone in this world. Many of us have been hurt, and more will be if we don't make noise.

I'll be the misfit. I always have been.

CHAPTER 4

She never came back

We trust who people tell us to trust. And why not? I lost so much that evening from trusting.

The next morning, my stomach growled almost as loudly as the new noise in my head. I had been left alone all night after being raped. (I didn't know the word yet.) But I knew I would never be the same, and I had to keep wiping my silent tears.

I remember smelling the bacon and saying out loud in a loud, irritated whisper, "She's making breakfast. What?" (Even right now, I feel the sadness and anger all at once, thirty years later.)

I waited as long as I could before leaving the room in which I'd become a different person in mere seconds (the first touch ruined me) and where I'd been left alone for the twelve hours that followed. I wasn't hungry until I smelled the food. I was, however, lonely. Leaning against the door on the floor for hours, I hoped any sound I heard was someone coming for me. I felt disgustingly different. I wasn't just physically sore. I was emotionally and mentally a wreck. I was ten.

I finally got up. I opened the door as quietly as I could. The normal creak of all the doors and wood floors made me jump for the first time ever. I crept through the halls, the same halls I'd just played hide-and-seek in the day before. I passed the now infamous couch I was stolen from only hours after sharing a bag of chips while watching Nickelodeon. Now everything felt like a spooky maze—filled with twists and turns someone might jump out of at any moment.

My thoughts berated me. Would I be made fun of or called a liar, as my own mother had eluded too? This was my first walk of shame, technically. My feelings were not even eleven years old, though, and my thoughts had no names or even full explanations.

Please speak to your children—no matter how much you don't want to. A child wouldn't make up something so horrific or, most importantly, scream. If you as a parent see part of your child's horror—no matter how guilty or afraid you feel—hold your baby first. I could tell you what I would do next to whoever hurt my baby, now that I'm a mother. However, it's not pretty.

I made it slowly to the kitchen, my heart pounding. It was in the middle of the house, down the longest hallway I've seen to this day, past the playroom and TV room, past a dining room that was never used. I followed the path leading to the center of the house, the kitchen. I stared at the flap doors. *Open them*, I yelled in my head. I didn't know what I would be facing on the other side. She never came back to check on me. Then I heard her. I opened the doors as she was coming around the corner from the guest area (where I usually stayed).

She was laughing with someone else I trusted. She smiled at me with a warning and came to my level, pretending nothing had happened. Through gritted teeth, she asked, "Want some eggs?

Really? I remember thinking.

I guess I needed a big dose of rape to understand the bullshit going on behind these walls. Soon, the reality of the world would hit me. I noticed everything, things I never did before—not in bright colors but, rather, more like dark shadows of truths all around me. I wouldn't understand facts until years and many therapeutic settings later.

I chose at that moment. I could cry and make a scene, or I could choose to be strong and well, a bitch to anyone who even tried to pretend or lie, behaviors I despise to this day.

Still ten, I felt different the next morning. I would very soon be very different. I still don't know where it came from—my sense, or this devious side I'd never had before. Before my mother's morning speech. You know the one given after your daughter was raped? Like it was normal or expected, I remember thinking. I realized people were fake, and nothing was ever as it seemed. Just days earlier, she'd held me close, playing with my hair. We were on the plane to America. It was a bumpy ride. She was telling me how much she loved me and hoped I'd never stop cuddling her. I didn't. But only days later, she would never cuddle me again.

To put it plainly. I never talked plainly about this until my late twenties and early thirties. I began to have bad dreams again and, thus, another relapse. Then everything was forced out of me during my seventh rehab.

The nightmares were always of me kicking and screaming (and still weeping silently). I do manage to say, "Shut up," in my nightmares.) That was absolutely what I was thinking then."

I am always in the same contorted position, still ashamed and scared. That makes it more of a nightmare than the actions that would paralyze me. Did he just ask, "Did I hurt you?"

I did turn my head in defiance that night. As he stumbled off about to get caught, I was numb. I remember thinking I wanted no one to see me cry from this day on, though I was weeping on tear-soaked sheets, and the pain between my legs was a pain I can't forget.

Shit happens, no one is perfect, just like this book. I have to "be careful what I say, and the truth." I am sick of everyone afraid of the truth.

It isn't surprising that the memory has always been intertwined with this horrific night. There's no question why. She, again, wasn't paying attention. I was alone.

Though children shouldn't ever be alone or feel unsafe. My reality and many paralyzed, sleepless nights awaken my menacing memory. I still clearly hear "her" emotionless orders to me. "It's only as bad as you make it."

These words have never left my memory, making me sick, some days.

It's true my children haven't always been proud of me because of my addiction and reckless choices. There is no excuse. I wrote my first unpublished book in mere weeks for my oldest daughter, "*Lyrics to Raquel*." I was twenty-two- and this was when my drug use had begun. And I was already apologizing for my poor choices. Trying to understand why and make sure my baby never blamed herself. She was my primary concern. It happened when there were no distractions, late at night, after a full day of my only happiness without my kids. Working in the studio, dancing, acting, or my modeling career. More importantly, there was the addiction to love. These addictions would plague me for decades with one man in particular. He and I would disappear, both lacking trust and better choices in life. However, when together, we were substance, we were our choice. Apart, we're a nightmare. Both still feared normalcy, reality, and abandonment.

He knew what to say. Protecting me from my anger, he validated me. However, he hated me when I went away to who I thought was stable. I was wrong. Humans are scary. We all have so much unhealed pain, and we take it out on those we love the most. It is a cliché, but it's the most truthful part of my life

I had been attending "the under belly" parties hidden in the hills full of dope since I was far underage. However, I was highly looked after. I was scared of substances and told not to touch them by my older brother, a crew of musicians my dad looked after. I went to these parties—whether it was the Grammys with my dad or friends. All the after-parties with friends and rock stars—as the parties could be nerve-racking, for me at times. It was part of my job.

Today, I am my children's only mother, and I have protected and loved them deeply. Sadly, my relapses would happen before each of my oldest daughters' tenth birthdays, after years of clean time.

I had been fighting my memories as hard as I could. Then my thirties hit, and my mind began unveiling more and more. It's actually more normal not to come out regarding your abuse until your thirties. This is particularly true for those who were treated like what happened to them was nothing or who were never believed, never revered.

This memory hounded me. It was at least an hour before I moved that night. The pain, fear, confusion, loneliness, and anger kept me pinned. Still, none of it compared to the horror I'd see when I finally stood up, facing myself—me alone and a dirty mirror. I still hate water marks on mirrors. Triggers are subtle, but they can ruin us.

Once ten-year-old me finally moved from the fetal position I would never be in today, I had to see if I looked different. I stood there in the dark for what seemed like forever. I could only see a shadow. It was fitting because Tamara was gone. I would go by my middle name Brooke from that day on. Of course my family still doesn't respect it fully. Family? Hmm.

Why do humans disrespect other humans and our space on this earth? It makes me sick to this day.

CHAPTER 5

Unconventional?

Here's my reality right now, as I type this up—along with spilling my coffee more times than I can count. The coffee is now cold and barely touched. These past weeks, I've been setting myself a deadline, so this will actually get done. I've even been allowing my son to eat snacks in bed, so I could focus with him close. I always need my children close. That's true no matter where this leads, speaking out about the worst things and the best.

I have started this book many times over the years. Also, I've typed aimlessly—the difference between then and now. I am allowing myself the space to release, without limits. I'm not just reminiscing, not just moving on. Rather, I'm healing and accepting; I am still overcoming.

I don't know how others write, type, or put thoughts on a page—in the end calling it a book, one someone will read, at least.

I can't worry myself with what you're thinking. We all have free will, and that's what makes life ultimately a great thing. I'm typing straight from within.

Sometimes, I feel like there's a gun to my head. I'm being ordered by a familiar voice. "This story must be told, even if no one cares at all." Are you turning the pages out of curiosity, need, or simply to criticize me? I wonder? Just a reminder; this is my life, my experiences. I lived on the edge, until I couldn't run anymore.

I must add, if anyone expects me to be conventional, I'd look at you like one of us was crazy. What is that anyway? How should we be? What shouldn't we be—sound easy? Conventional, as defined in the dictionary is, "Based on or in accordance with what is generally done or believed."

Sounds like a death sentence to me—worse than boring, invoking expectations no one can live up to. How depressing, to wake up and think, *I'm conventional. Like a bloody pot roast in an oven.*

CHAPTER 6

Twisted Trauma Hostage

Jump to That is what unhealed trauma will do. You think it's fixed, somehow it gets sticky like glue or a magnet that sick people got stuck to back in the day."

Here we go:

The doorbell rang, and it was one of Tiger's runners with a key to a spot he had further down Piedmont. It was well furnished, and his sister slept in the third room. But his whole family ran a drug empire that went through restaurants, dry cleaners, and numerous dope runners in no less than a fifteen mile radius running to and from each street and regulars always in their daily crooked parking dope sick position. How I drove through this life for the first years. While I occasionally did the corner runner rounds for Tiger. He had a few of us "college looking girls" go check on the runners. I would have books and wear glasses, in case we were pulled over. Why? Because a girl who looked like me in this bluffy area, stuck out like a sore thumb. More than once I was pulled over. Once it happened to me with a chick who I used smack with daily. She couldn't figure out how my veins were so quick and clean? Whilst I was more worried about getting pulled over again. It was different every time we got pulled over in my white Lexus SUV in the worst area at the edge of the city. (known for crime, dope, few were allowed all the way in without a gun pointed at you or being shot on the spot.) Tiffany and I made friends anywhere we went and never minded watching these runners like clockwork. I watched the same orders daily, one in particular from a regular. Every morning by eight a.m. (I said it was like a job) the same sweaty addict who I saw every morning and always thought to myself, Brooklin if you get to a point you can't afford more than a day or for sure my morning shot. Drag yourself to get clean, ugh."

Speaking of, I was starting to feel sick, (such an awful addiction) It was a job in itself. I didn't see it that way then. Good thing because my heart was suddenly beating like rapid fire as I suddenly wasn't as confident about the cop (still) approaching. Shit "Tiffany" what do I say again when he approaches? I hear her tapping her neck for a vein, then arms, and gruntinting. I look over. "Really Tif?" Dude? She is sweating profusely herself. My eyes started to vibrate and I am sure my pupils are up to no good if the cocky cop finally gets to my window and will he notice." "Tiffany" is itching now. "Ugh we are such junkies." She says. Me, "Shhh, Jesus, don't say it out loud and especially as a cop is slowly sauntering up." As I was him checking out my plate and car from my rear view mirror. He is certainly wondering why two well dressed girls are in this area and at eight a.m. Beside my fear of his flashlight, every runner and a few grandmas who cook the dope behind the flap where her nephew, Son, nephew, y'all I have been served by boys not much older than eight? A grandson learning the business. It was lucrative, I wanted to ask why the shacks, rats and, furthermore, why live in the bluff? Easy answer from contention I have rarely felt. Why not, if we don't sell, someone else will, a toothless sweet old lady known as "Auntie." Still waiting for the cop as he seemed uncomfortable with the entire outside, usually hidden or busy bees working, were still and staring straight at us. Did they know we were being tested? Or even the coo? "Tiffany, do you care if this cop is slow?" "No, but yo yo he may be as slick as the dude looking at me" "I look and see a huge man with a 45 round cocked in his mind." His eyes were in between bitch this is when we know why you are "creepin" in around this hood side by side almost daily. Falling apart more and more, I see the flashlight. She was irritated with her

Thigh Highs and No Lies

veins and was annoyed I was always springing mine in seconds. "Not now Tif." "I drove and shot up dope in less than a minute, looking back I am not proud of any of that, but it kept me from being in agony like Tif when we had to keep together. The cop finally made it to my window and asked "girls are you ok?" Me, "No Sir, I am new at Tech and I am lost?" The cop said, "Girls, you have to get out of this area, and I look scared and he gives us two turns and a direct way to campus. Did it work every time? Yes, that did.

However, Soon I would have lost everything again at twenty-eight. I got clean and got pregnant with my third healthy baby girl. I did get bored when she started preschool and needed help staying up for the college courses I was taking. That brought me to a gas station on the way to school one morning. Scout started talking to me. He had seen me before and the needles in my open dash. He noticed everything. At first, I was a target, a friend and we had a strong partnership and connection. He just got out of prison the night we met, opening the back door while my head was down looking for lipgloss. There was silence, usually Baldhead is chatting me up by now. I slowly go from his dark blue rubber sandals (newly out of prison, not jail. check) eyes slowly moving past the gun tucked in sight and my smile still wide without flinching. He later would tell me he appreciated that and knew I would be his number one. "Brooklin was back in business, damn it!" You aren't half in or out of this life. I became his biggest money-making venture over the next three years before I got clean for good.

Madame please:

Slim was our first girl, and she met a few through parties I set up for rich men in high-rise hotels that required a key to go up. Never ever go to a hotel where the doors are on the outside. Change when you get there or wear a classy coat and, in the summer, a maxi dress with your garters and "whatnots" hidden.

On both sides of the United States I did this with the same rules. I had stunning women who were "models" who needed more to round up their "way of life." They all had wants—whether headshots and a place to stay or the chance to find a rich husband. Yet, almost a decade older and modeling again, even a recent Maxim Cover. Yet, life is in suburbia now. that must be told. I mean maybe. Or am I just bold, it isn't enough to be stuck here?

These memories have been swirling like a hawk and, of course, on the day I am only supposed to organize these damn chapters. The hardest part—these memories came up and wouldn't let up. So here we are in the darkest moments of my life, while I was still sportin' nice cars and a persona that was barely hanging on. The last minute, adding my vivid picture for you? Why? Idk? It's where trauma took me.

However, today thoughts that do the back stroke through my mind, with rainbows and puddles my kids can jump in endlessly while I glide through the water knowing all is well. Don't just play. Don't just lay. Don't just think of yesterday. Don't just learn, experience.

> Don't just read, absorb.
> Don't just change, transform.
> Don't just relate, advocate.
> Don't just promise, prove.
> Don't just criticize, encourage.
> Don't just think, ponder.
> Don't just take, give.
> Don't just see, feel.
> Don't just dream, do.
> Don't just hear, listen.
> Don't just talk, act.
> Don't just tell, show.
> Don't just exist, live.
> DON'T just ANYTHING!
> Especially waiting. For what?
> The time is now.

CHAPTER 7

The Good Parts Please

(Daddy)

To the good parts please. I always wake up and call my dad if he hasn't called me already. He calms me. He calls me "Cookie", which I love. I am beyond grateful my Dad became my Father. God sends you so much you will never expect. I can promise you that.

But it was Dave, Dad, who saved my life, and it would be quite a bit later when I would find out he happened to be famous. He did make all my dreams as a Father figure and a Daddy realized. As far as my career, he made me work for that. I had to audition for everything I did. I hope anyone hurting knows this—*your pain will lead you to a destiny you can't even imagine.*

Here we go: Flashback (This used to happen almost daily)

Still, there's the memory of when I sat up and touched my tanned, tiny inner thighs—peeking under my big T-shirt, past the tan lines of a formerly happy summer. There were spots of blood on the beige sheet under the pristine white floral covers. That's when reality hit me. I was no longer a little girl. It would be twenty-two years before I would be told I had been raped.

It would be more than a decade before I would be able to even choose to go beyond journaling and occasionally speaking publicly on "abuse and neglect," still not quite identifying with what had happened to me being a rape. Why not? It is such a reality. Incidentally, it is now August. Oh and worse, last month the evening news reported on a ten-year-old girl who was reportedly granted an abortion after she was raped by her uncle. It was confirmation that I should not fear my story being told and the same month of my rape.

Once we finally make emotionally peace with the facts, most importantly, we must remain kind. We must hold onto the knowing deep down that we are not the reason for their poor choices to hurt us. It is our responsibility not to hurt back. However, don't hide it all so deeply that you forget your strengths and weaknesses and keep yourself from knowing who you are at all. That almost killed me.

As a teen, I would spend many days dazed, half awake, carving words on desks, tagging walls and trains. Was I trying to say what I felt somehow? Ultimately, it is my t wasn't my job to help myself. I was a child—one who was told that enduring terrible abuse wasn't that bad; move on. Life isn't one experience; it's many. However, I knew this one experience, at ten, would shape me forever.

What has shaped you?

Caged you even?

CHAPTER 8

Flying Saucers in My Mind

I hope that even as I somehow explain how, everyday life—what was normal for others—used to become obsessions for me. Or the opposite would be the case; I wouldn't give a damn. I'm obsessed with helping others, even if it means losing my own opportunities and dreams. It helped me focus on what strengths I knew I had. It gave me purpose in life. I'm talking about the dreams we daydream of as a kid while in math class, staring aimlessly out the window. Back then, even before I was ten and before the ultimate betrayal, my view was mountains. We lived in the Valley. Luckily, I was good at compartmentalizing and some of those daydreams did come true. Especially if grown and aware you are trying to help others with your deepest trauma, you are brave for speaking up. Forget those who walk away.

I remember my own mother walking away. She looked directly into my big, usually bright blue eyes, now bloodshot. And for a split second, I saw her shock, even pain, certainly fear. Was she unsure how to respond to me? How? As a mother now, I could never ever not respond in that situation.

One minute, I cared, and the next, I'd forget I had ever given a fuck. Today, there's a name for it—*ghosting*. Back then, in the '90s and 2000s, we just stopped calling or receiving calls. Before text was a thing, relationships were much simpler. However, I do wish there were camera phones, recordings, and shit. Even Google would have enabled me to look up what had happened to me at ten. I was clueless.

I will be talking about life in Hollywood below. It's bizarre. But first I had to stop skipping around and tell you the absolute most perverted, stomach-curdling moment in my life. It was my first brush with death (emotional death, that is).

You'd think accomplishing my larger-than-life dreams would make it all go away one day. Or you might think having money would cure my past. Nothing does, except truth, love, and acceptance.

Remember this. They've had trauma too, and you reminded them of a time they had no one either. Trauma is hard to face. It's like not knowing what to say when your friend loses a family member. Even if we couldn't imagine, we're frozen.

Today there are resources for everything, and we care and believe every word you say. The beginning of healing is feeling heard.

Breathe. You aren't alone in this world. Many of us have been hurt, and more will be if we don't make noise.

I'll be the misfit.

I always have been.

Chapter 9

Feeling Fucked? It All Matters

Does this matter?
What the fuck have I done?
I have loved.
I have hurt.
Haven't we all?
I have fucked,
And I have been fucked up
And fucked over…
What kinda poetry is this shit?
Mine. Write what you feel. If it rhymes,
Yay, ring a damn bell.
Most importantly, you all matter.
So let's do a restart

It all matters,
Even the days I spent in jail thinking I was going to prison.
Those days mattered.
Now when *it* counts,
I slouch and have bouts of obsessions. Who counts in your life?
We all do, fuckers!

***

Sorry. Some stop and become judgmental and choose. Quit being square and unfair. Trust me. None of us is worth being treated less than for caring, sharing, or believing in you. I assure you fewer than you think do.

So before you cross, block, or try and forget you knew they breathed and laughed or even made you smile, remember, few give a fuck if you died tomorrow.

Your circle is smaller than you think.

We are set up to fail; it is up to us to fucking prevail. There's your rhyme.

This book is a clusterfuck, just like life has seemed. It has beautiful and surreal moments. Yet, still, there are moments so ugly they destroy many.

Bruh, they are just real people.

So, these are some who would be presumed famous.

Bruh, they're just real people.

Watch out now because they start to believe in the *fame*tasy themselves.

I've lost a lot of friends over their newfound *fame*tasy, forgetting they couldn't pay their rent a year before.

No, I won't tell you whose rent I paid. It didn't matter to me then. I had my pad and could afford theirs too. Life flips in the business—like Saturday morning gluten-free pancakes with cocoa and turmeric golden milk. We cleanse our insides with green juice and never swallow anything with preservatives. Back home, We take a few bites and push our plate away. Maybe it's because that's how I was raised. Don't finish your plate; eat less.

To this day, I eat to live, not live to eat. Thank God, because forty stole my teenage metabolism straight from under me. As I was or wasn't, here we are.

Editing is a bitch, and I may not always make sense in tandem,. But this was the next sentence. (Basicaf lol)

First, about my imperfect way of typing these thoughts, memories, and lyrics at times. It's how I speak my mind.

The key is definitely the right timing.

I still sit alone, not lonely. Though I'm ready for this book to stop calling me back after I have sent more than a handful of "finished manuscripts to my publishers."

Like my children, I want to get it right.

My children are so beautiful.

That's a lot to ask. Let's just tell you how life happened, and I ended up here—talking to you, myself, and those who know who they are. A few have come from my womb. I've made many mistakes in life.

But not any are my babies.

***

Are you really ready to read about the almost rise with plenty of falls and then some?

Maybe—as you read this mezzo mix, including the story of my years in the business, after landing in Hollywood very young—you'll be wondering, Who the hell is who?

Years later here I am, in and out.

Some old friends will, without a doubt, think, "Brooklin, *shit, she's alive, she survived?*"

"She's actually still alive."

Yah, yeh of little faith I am!

"Brooklin doesn't lay down and die regardless"

All my memories are rolled into stories.

Which is how my memories are so vivid, that and journals since I was eleven.

I have not wanted to use the word *stories*, as it implies fiction to many. These are memories rounded up into story form so one can understand how we got from here to there. Sometimes I fail.

What you see is what you get.

Love, you mean it.

Break.

CHAPTER 10

Decades of Lives Lived

Before I learned how to heal without involving anyone.

I feel stupid for needing anyone. But I did then. Now I need the light to turn out and your face to open the door where you fixed the blackout and you see in my face, don't say anything by "must have been the circuit break.

Don't Leo that shot again, it's a nightmare. You and your monkey wrench is a toddlers. Oh right, sorry about that, I was making a point. Toddlers go through phases, and I'm sorry. You are the last person I would have ever chosen to be nothing but an enemy, but you did, so dedicated to more trauma and lack of trust. As I picked out my new home in noho, I thought- awe this fucker.

Nice! I was scared for too many years, you took so long to just be. I wasn't enraged by our time apart, I was broken from my life and had done really well at pretending it was what it was.

Then there is what I should have realized was the real me.
Being someone's break, or someone being mine, and laughing in our private regular no pressure moments. I can't remember until this year every talking about us EVER!

No expectations
I can't believe we both made it this far.

If rejection is your fear, well fuck that's a risk you take to
Stop the rain and the black cloud from silly clowns deep down making it hard to keep it together in this town.

Sound check one, two…

Few or many in between breaks and yet we circle back after time, or even a misunderstanding, leading to a crash and burnt heart. We take the leap, and the smile at the man most would be turned off by the simple moments grab -

REMEMBER: MOMENTS MAKE OR BREAK US. EVERYTHING WE HAVE GONE THROUGH.
Think about the make it or break it moments.

THEY LEAD YOU TO YOU AND ARE THE MOST RAW AND MEMORABLE.
CONVENTIONAL OR SIMPLE.
MOMENTS MATTER -
PLEASE GRAB THEM.

Hint- Hurt- always tell them- when you have them face to simply. And the spark with reignite. It's hiding your blockage in that moment you know you have to grab.
Don't be afraid.
That day I didn't have a spark and tried to tell you, I love you there and everywhere, except when I feel so small because I fruitcake, because "little nightmare" for giving up and saying "no worries, it's cool"
"be there in ten"
Omg wth?
"I am too kind I guess?"

BtwI I'm "your litttle" nightmare.
Made me giggle.
Then a song filled with our texts wrapped into one was released. But it hurt.

The blackout.

"Never just hello and goodbye with us ever" he says.

Dude time is fucking theif.

Took me years to come back home.
Like you asked, now here and…memories jog through me most, as you were a constant over many years. Moments I always grabbed with satisfaction and by my kid 29's accepted them for the long or short of them.

I have changed since this book and my other projects too, my freedom, and starting over at forty one alone.
No expectations
Meeting up if you should pass up toddler tools and ikea furniture building with Swedish rules.
Directions are for fools.
Leaning at the door and peeking in, what will you see?

Leaving home studio bound, will required to put on clothes.
Doable.
And Break.

Back in the decades of my late teens and 20's:

My fits of rage would come out of nowhere, and I couldn't control them. I was on anxiI left home with my Mothers's blessing before my fifteen birthday. That was the extent of our communication until I was well over eighteen. I was fighting my grief. Missing the baby I lost, I knew I would never raise, I realized I had to know if I would be running forever. If I could go back in time, if I could fix it all, I would protect my choices, without fear.
I had complete freedom by the spring, as a legal young adult. heading back to The Hills. I had no one to answer to. Some screams still echoed after midnight with flashbacks. Paralyzing nightmares he

would wake me up when I couldn't get out. He broke through my wall and U didn't want to make him feel responsible to save me. I usually lay silently still tears soaking my pillow on my side of the bed. As I tried to breathe normally and not wake him all at once. I was strong and loved for now. Enjoy it damn it Brooklin

Some nights I was sweaty and afraid. My boyfriend would wake me and console me. No one knew what happened to me eight years earlier. Except the bits I had felt he need to know. He never seemed to judge me. He has lately for things I haven't done. Or he perceived me wrong for the first time, that it would break our unique bond.

There were breaks and lots of studio time, both places I thrived. In ninety nine, after a short tour, someone suggested I make peace with my mom—even as I'd scream at her in my nightmares. On protest, yet clearly easily controlled, I flew at eighteen to where my mother was "then" to a completely separate life.

This seemed to be a constant for me. Soon after I'd arrived, I saw clearly that my mother was still the same, and I wasn't. Though, I was tired. Within days, I attempted suicide and almost succeeded. I spent ten days in the ICU. Yo never be that fucking insecure, selfish and weak.

This upset so many who loved me. So came across the country to cry or yell. Sneaking in and out, not to be seen. For both our sakes. You handful saved my future. Will you again as I am coming home after about deathly feeling, not seeing my children daily. I am broken. Will anyone be there for me?

Why did I deserve it then, and I turn forty and I have less support, though I am more reliable and that stupidity replaced with years of experiences becoming wisdom.

To my surprise, my mother was terrified of me almost dying. She did help me shower during my two-week haze. She even chose for me to go with her to her home, instead of returning to the model apartment attached to my talent agency. She knew exactly why I was breaking down—what memories I was suppressing. On the car ride leaving the hospital, all I could think of is why did it have to come to this for her to take the initiative to be a mom to me? She had not spoken to me in over three years. As a mother now, I would never not speak to my children between fifteen and eighteen when they need their Mom the most.

By now, my dad was in my life and understood me It was time to go home to Noho. I missed my life as a dancer as well as the man I loved. He didn't understand how I clung to him yet would leave for what turned out to be a couple years. Over two decades it would be a roller coaster of two men, me, and all my babies and the other baby Momma's. Common in this Industry

Chapter 11

Neon

The back of my mind has always had big neon signs flashing all the time. Even when dreaming, what's wrong with the neon signs in the back of my mind? Telling me it was my fault. It wasn't me the night I lost everything I ever knew at ten. In a town where everything you see has to be altered to become what they want you to be. For me, inevitably, I still saw neon inside me. When I was younger, my dreams were big and actually happening—they were neon too.

Do we all fit where we ended up?

Did I scare myself away? Thus pushing you to your breaking point.

I know many who gave their lives to rock and roll. Now looking back, the "I love yous" silently mouthed to me by "him"—the one everyone swore I would make whole. "You are so good for him. You both see the same way." You mean in neon lights?

However, I am no longer there to see the damages from years lost, all the costs of the lives we lived separately, as the neon signs faded with the army behind me and the party once in front of me. I wasn't alone. But I stayed wandering with the wrong one. I became less jaded as I released the access and realized the moments that matter had one thing in common. Freedom of me and whomever it concerned: I still tried to bring normalcy, though I know my frustration gets the best of me when too far from home. I'm growing up before judgment day, it will be OK. But thenI realize no environment matters, I thrive at home in Hollywood. I die a slow death in the petri dish of this city of the south that will never ever be what just walking around my city does for my spirit in a minute. Waking up to the Symbol of my town, with the silence of the loud bright sun setting over the name that people flock to. As my coffee's aroma silently envelopes me, my soundtrack for the day begins and it usually dictates how it's gonna go. That and to follow through, not fearing anything from the moment I get home. My second act is worth more than my first, I was given a lot by being young and talented. Was it the young or the talent. We will know soon.

    It's lonely in my mind sometimes, as I fill these pages with my past. It's time to let it all go and focus.
    Time's a thief; don't waste it on neon signs like me. It keeps you from being free. stop wasting it on neon signs in our minds.
    Look clearly at those who stick around and how they make you feel. If you miss them, tell them. If you feel you should apologize for being cruel, then do so.
    Take this from someone who just lost her stepfather days ago out of the blue. Say what you have to say. Go to one last show. Who cares what they do? This is about you.

CHAPTER 12

Flashbacks

Jump to when I was working at Lethal Dose's—auditioning, modeling, and walking through red ropes. I was working by Dad's side, partying and in studios by night.

In between dancing on tours, I stayed in the crew, and danced part time at the Viper Room as a burlesque dancer. I was invited to Carmen's rehearsal dinner. By a twist of fate, I sat down and was face-to-face with "him."

I was actually dating someone else in the industry. However, no one understood (nor did I) how he always took priority. Before I could process his dark brown puddles of lies, at the time, you could have told me shit was the prettiest sky. (I do love brown eyes to this day and his.)

Carmen ran over in five-inch heels, five three to my five eight. Her long, highlighted, shiny Rita Hayworth hair bounced with her. She hugged me and screamed "God, Brooklin, you are the most beautiful woman I swear." Your family's genetics, girl."

You know that moment when all the clanking of cutlery, plates, chatter, even the DJ A.M. skipped a beat—silence.

Joseph's a restaurant was a decent size, in the heart of the bottom of the hill. However, unless you were a native or a successful entertainer, you'd drive right by. A restaurant by day, it was a wild club by night. As the music and chatter started back, I mouthed, "Award," to "him," who was sitting directly behind Carmen's bear hug around me with what smirk of his, and I believe, a chicken wing in his mouth. I rolled my eyes with a laugh and felt less uneasy. I squeezed her perfectly tight body, no phoniness there, and thanked her for having me and, of course, told her she was nuts, Goddess. Women supporting women has always warmed my gut.

    The place was full. Most of us knew each other. The inner circle of this town is so small. I knew everyone, Musicians frequented my dad's office or studios daily. If you didn't know someone at a private party such as this, you learned quickly to mingle. The hills are fickle. If you don't stay in the loop, like a cowboy with a lasso, catches those who have other destinies and throws us aside. Yup, even me for a while. And I was born in and for this industry. Some forever, me here and there. Where am I now? Here and there, literally.

    After that moment, I was twenty-one and in the loop. However, in the loop or not, I had a wedgie in my perfectly tailored leather pants. Fuck. Carmen, cover me."

    But as quick as she was just there, she was gone. So I grabbed Rob. let me tell you, leather pants and wedgies are better left untouched. Yet, he paused and covered me laughing as I tried to be classy. Digging out a widgie is anything but, I shouldn't have worn panties anyway. I must have anticipated a moment in time that was due. Every two to three years, our eyes would meet.

    I finally heard my favorite voice beside me with that Valley twang and his bossy thang, kindly using my nickname from him, near my ear he spoke with a smile and I know you wonder how I would know. If you're blessed you just do. No matter what that love looks like or doesn't. Either way as he spoke those syllables, my whole body reacted for the first time in over a year. I instantly remembered the soberness of this intoxication. Even now I feel the electricity going up my spine, the stimulation that only he could create in me on just utterly few words. He could do the same staring at me saying everything, without a spoken word.

    A Moment I would grab, as I swirled around and looked up and he grabbed my hands and mouthed "Let's go". We didn't have to worry anymore if anyone saw.

"Sky Blu," he proudly announced, "you're home and grown. Can't wait to get you home."

Yea that was a long time ago. But then while fiddling through my bag for ChapStick. I stopped abruptly, yet looked up slyly, knowing my eyes would affect him. Why? Everyone knew me for my seea-blue almond eyes. There is more behind these blue eyes, as a Friend says.

That "November" night, it had been almost two years apart and seven years since we'd innocently met, "him" and I., Even if our last moments were left messy, we always forgave. Something changed recently and it scares me. Am I not good enough, or too real and aware, too grown? This evil feeling comes over me. I react with a tear and uncontrollable shiver.

Lastly, I pray he listens to the right verse that is always playing or he is writing in his mind throughout his days in or out of the studio. Hell isn't in my eyes, two bodies come alive and there two humans laugh the more we make the choice to be ourselves. Which is hard when there isn't stability. Now I am home.

Nothing to hash out or anyone to tell. I will always know him.

As I write this book of memories, my memories of him hurt and are the most to me all at once. I smile with hope, I also deflate with fear as he may choose to risk the moments I know grabbing will change us both. Not expectation wise. Knowing we matter. And we cross paths for a reason.

Being provoked by the one time and our last interaction, so foreign to our silly banter and sexual nature. It was time for a change. I wasn't ready to try something new and let go or 22 me and always older, yet 22 too you. That day we were projecting frustration and fear.

Which wouldn't matter if you peaked in my new place in Noho, when an address pops up on your screen.

Will he beam and go with it as he used to, or stop and over think the moment that we both need.

He doesn't know how I do. Is Simply the ability to never get too angry, not drop him, because what is inside me is eternal and has chosen a few to never give up on.

He always asked the same thing. "Are you back to live here for good?"

This time I am. Will he be able to show his happy

And sit next to me while I use toddler tools to put together IKEA furniture or maybe I will wait and be working in a tee and sheer bottoms. My legs hopefully are not bruised, but no promises.

Back then, I had control. I lost that as soon as I began this book and realized I Was forty and still not home and where I Wanted to be personally. Makes me angry. But I am close. Though, this book turned me upside down for a while. I got stuck in my 20's. To all those I overwhelmed, some still here, some not, some who may come back, forgive me for being too much and overwhelmed. I dreaded this task for twelve years. When I was asked to write this book—from my pain and humiliation to my absolute wild hysteria and excitement to the mundane.

I just wanted some of it back—the time I mean. Like this memory, I get lost, intoxicated by deep thoughts. Then like a daydream ending when the bell rings, I am interrupted by my present thoughts and dwelling on loss. Forgetting isn't easy for me. As a writer, I see things differently, clearly.

Like most women, my story isn't as different as many may think. As we all go through pain. The closure we miss, when the person we love turns on us. It isn't me he's hurting from. Timing is everything. Forgive those who hurt you. Treat people kindly. Even when the truth in your words may hurt, assert your cause.

Pause.

Be that break—not the breakdown. You are worthy, and so is the person who hurt you.

CHAPTER 13

Junkie with a Capital J

I am not afraid to be clear. I was a junkie. Years later came the first time I used heroin. I had a friend who shall remain nameless—rest in peace. I had him shoot me up. I spent the next eight years fighting with heroin and many times out loud. Why? Why? Why?

If anyone out there is fighting, I will tell you why. That shit gets in your bones and slowly steals your soul. If you go too far, it takes your heart too.

First came clear—or "crystal" to some. But I hated the feeling of being so up and talking even more. Ugh!. So then came the pills. I had a back injury, so it wasn't hard to get pills. With that, and at this time being married to an NBA player, doctors gave me anything. I always had bottles of up to 250 painkillers on me. This is when I accidentally became a dealer for the first time. I just gave them away, because I didn't need them all.

Did I see myself as that at the time? No. Just like I didn't know I was an addict or, later, a madam. I was absolutely in denial and had the finances to continue for many years.

After four and a half semi-functioning years, I finally went to my first treatment center. My addiction staggered through years of trying to get well. Yet, I always got up, I never stayed down for long. I went to many places for help and education on addiction. And lastly, for sexual trauma, an internationally known doctor sent me to a trauma center where my life would change forever.

This is where I would finally figure out It wasn't until the root was ripped out that I would begin my healing and, at thirty-three, did stay clean. It was also soon after that my then eight-year-old daughter was diagnosed with cancer. If anything is going to keep you straight, it's almost losing a child. I am going to end with this, because all the details—from arrests, to being rich, then back to the trap house life. I don't matter, is all I thought for years. What matters is they were all my choices. My choices. However, I did matter and had someone invested in truly making sure I knew that night wasn't my fault or sat me down, versus feeding my addiction with cash and full accounts. Just maybe this charade wouldn't have lasted so long.

I have lost so many friends to overdose. There are only three places you will end up—institutions, jail, or death.

You aren't alone if you are struggling, escaping life and pain with drug abuse. I promise you, there is something in you that needs healing. And right now, stop looking down on yourself or allowing anyone else to do so. You are human. And no one can say they don't do something when no one is looking that society would deem shameful. Ignore what others think.

Many years later, the rush of shooting heroin was my remedy for fading these memories, if only for a while. Ultimately, it is just more pain and poison you are allowing to take over your reality—and soon you. Whether your belief in the severity of what happened to me is a choice, your choice. This book will uncover what was buried. Those aren't my main reasons for writing this book. Nor is it my problem if it feels like an attack. The truth hurts. Lies hurt worse. That night, I changed—not just that night but forever. And that impact remains a part of me now as I continue to heal and remind myself of mine and all of our worth. My own worth means me being in a place where this book will be given more than thoughts but, rather, wings to fly—fly away from my prison with a key for yours truly, I pray.

We have to begin anything before it's accomplished. It sounds simple, but that's the hardest part. When writing a book about your life experiences, the hardest part for me is knowing when to let some memories go. Which ones matter? First, you will have a goal—whether it be purely money for your work or motives of the heart.

Both are important. Motivation has to come from different places sometimes. Giving up was not an option this time, whereas I have given up on two other books before. This time, the fire in me is lit.

After all the years of feeling less than and being told, in fact, "You'll never finish anything," those words have become my motivation. Find the key that opens the door to exactly who you want to be or what you want to see every day when you wake up. Lock that door tight so no one else sees and hold that key and vision tight. That is how you start anything—with a dream and the fight to keep going. My whole life has been a fight, many would say a dream too. I agree. I have been blessed. However, had I been healed, I would have realized my worth while I was there and wouldn't have gotten stuck in life's what-ifs? My dad says, "Life is what is in the middle *if*."

But Brooklin, *what if* you did it? Perhaps if you didn't, that feels worse than if it does well over never knowing. So how to do anything, for me, is to not live on the outskirts of life anymore—never again. It's life in the now, the *if* of it all.

There are a few things I never wavered on and followed through. Being a dancer was my first true freedom. Writing came soon thereafter. And then there was having my beautiful children. I never wavered on wanting children and to be a mother—even after seeing evil face-to-face in a mother. It didn't erase my dream to hold my true loves, my children.

CHAPTER 14

Red-Light District

Living with demons is like standing in the middle of the red-light district at twelve, with my mom. I knew this wasn't exactly tourism. I wondered, *Why am I here? What am I supposed to be learning from this?* In the back of my mind were the big neon signs we see all over the red-light district. I am very visual. And like all memories, going through that district of nude women, addicts, and bright neon signs saying anything you may want was like electricity. Well, if you want to fuck a stranger who may be full of disease but that seems better than a clean woman with expectations? Wankas. It always puzzled me why so many take that risk, not to love. All of this was going through my twelve-year-old mind. I was breathless from keeping up with my mom on a mission. Literally.

Mother took me there for the first time at twelve. Also, the red-light district was, to her, a "must-see." She said, "These people live like this all day and night. You have such a good life."

I knew I did. That's why it took me so long to write this book. I'm not whining. I'm simply telling the truth, hopefully so others will suffer less.

The sign flashes, though it is less bright. The word failure is flashing less than it did yesterday. It's still there, though, in neon green. It accompanies the compulsive thought always plaguing me, running a marathon in my head. *"You will fail, and no one will care."* The further I go, or rather, the more I type, towards somewhere, at the end, the sign fades. The more I power through, the sign even starts falling. Is it the wind or my dedication?

I always wondered if my mom opened my eyes to dark places so I'd know they existed everywhere. Most importantly, perhaps she wanted me to know they weren't just in my head or that guest room bed just two year earlier. She was too drunk to save me then. I wish that weren't true. As a mom, even if I were drunk, trust, don't touch my child.

Does that time matter? No it never did. Not ever, to my mom. Whatever kept her free or me sidetracked mattered to her.

My mom was passionate, too, and she helped many. It wasn't all bad; she got a high of amazing perks and peaks into other ways of life through her work.

The Wall came down when I was eight. I saw the freedom flowing through these Germans just a walk a way, still in fear. I wonder now, was there any help for PTSD for them? Probably not? Heartbreaking.

She took me all over Europe and made sure I saw the world—especially refugee camps. We went close to the borders to bring provisions since I was young. It changed me to see people running free and yet still afraid. After the Wall came down, these brave families running away from genocide, yes genocide STILL in the 1990s.

America had no clue what was happening across those wild seas. Few Americans know about the Wars still tearing families and countries apart. I was proud of *"Blood and Honey" by Ang*. Somebody cared. It was a real and wonderfully deep film depicting exactly what my mom's purpose was for being there. She was trying to save nations. That's what I did know.

I remember my mom taking me to eastern block countries when we went less than a year after the wall came down, we stayed at a beautiful hotel that was finally being restored. However, all they had to eat was liver and dumplings in broth. There was still a bread shortage, no matter if we had money. My mother taught us to be equals and that they needed it more than us. I did admire my mother for many things—just not mothering, though she will probably agree with that fact.

I realize all these great things she exposed me too and accomplished on her own also affected me. I remember my face wet from tears and, eventually, sweat trying to help new refugees coming to the border from their war-torn countries. Many of my American friends had no idea. There's plenty of third world existence right in beautiful castle-filled Europe.

I have many memories of no one noticing or caring. Though I was a child wandering around in the middle of such chaos, I knew this was wrong. Why was no one helping? I wanted to know, to understand. But most of all, I wanted to help.

I threw myself into helping anytime mom or my stepdad would take me to a refugee camps. I flourished in helping others. Even my mother noticed that character trait in me when I was very young and acknowledged it. That meant a great deal to me. You see, her acknowledgement happened so little.

However, by the time I was twelve, I was bucking the system, the fairy tale my mother thought she'd created and the nightmare she hoped I'd forgotten happened. I hadn't forgotten, and the nightmare wouldn't end for decades. I know life isn't perfect. It's not supposed to be. However, so much being done or ignored is just wrong and has to stop. If I have to be the first one to say, "I was raped at ten by someone I knew and trusted," I will; I am.

Certainly, my mother didn't care about healing or even listening, much less holding me and, no matter what her mind said, telling me, a child who was traumatized, "It's going to be OK, baby girl." She preferred to mutter, "Dry it up," "I'm sleeping," or, "Quit the bullshit."

When I'd wake up terrified from a nightmare from my past, I would sit in the door frame of my room—a floor below her in our tall house in Europe. I would cry myself to sleep in my doorway, waking up there defeated. Every rejection of my pain from her, left another wound. Did she not know, as a mother, she had the superpower of love that could cure much of my pain? She never came to get me or talk to me. She never played with my hair again, like she had before "that night." I still didn't understand and kept fighting for her to hear me. Anytime I did have nightmares, all I wanted was a hug. It doesn't take long to start looking for love, recognition, or attention outside the home. So I did. Dancing was where I put most of my energy, and I stuck it out.

Skip to age seventeen. I was dancing part-time at dance studios in the valley. I had been obsessed with dance since I was six on the army bases, until my teens. Though training was tedious, I never wanted to leave my dance classes. Dancing was where I felt worth anything at all. Remembering those times wakes my spirit—as it did then. We all need passion and a purpose. We all have more than one also.

When I was young, I was confused. Yet, I dated men, not boys. I always wanted to be protected, to learn, and to be loved. I had little supervision, and my mother had no clue where I was. We didn't speak for over three years. When I became pregnant by an older man and wanted to keep the baby, she threw me out for the second time. I left and never looked back.

Chapter 15

Needles and Shallow Breathing

I fought hard to hold on to my pain, using every substance. It was all I had that felt real for years. Unlike some who run from trauma, I had to understand, even then. However, This led to me eventually becoming a heroin addict. We have to get help, talk to someone who understands and cares. It took years to get me there. I chose to be an overachiever first, dancing professionally at age seventeen, working in studios that I dreamed of. The adrenaline kept my heart pumping for years. Then my thirties hit.

We aren't there, yet. First, I had to come to terms with how hard I loved—everyone but myself of course. For many years, I didn't realize it was a blessing in disguise. The way I love took the few I did by surprise. Once I love you, you can do no wrong, ride or die. I will be there until the end. However, there are few I love at all or deeply. All my loves are different, some friends and the few that were lovers. It didn't matter how it went up or down. I never left anyone I loved, unless I was on drugs.

CHAPTER 16

Hooked: Shit, Let's Write a Book

Like a song, this hook replays in my mind.

How do you write a fucking book? I mean without losing your mind? Recently added, as days have passed, but I haven't given up.

I'm living and breathing whatever this will end up being. Honestly, it's hardest for me to please myself. So, I doubt I will ever feel done. But I'm here, starting sentences from the rear at times. Am I just typing for my sanity?

Here we are, all the noise around me and in my head. I guess that's the theme. It's all in my head? That's where the reel has been sitting, collecting dust. Sometimes, it's haunting me, until I decided to start typing.

I woke up and just started typing. Thus, it's becoming a book. At least, I think.

Before I had brain scans, mainly to see if I was healed from all my bad choices—aka intense drug use. I've added the results at the end, the very last pages.

Science is what pumped me up—finding out the truth. One of those truths was that my mother had me convinced I was going mad since I was twelve (convenient timing). I felt I was losing it for years. I let it go because I'm actually the one in control.

You are *not alone*.

I remember feeling so alone all the time. I believe they were hurt too.

CHAPTER 17

Need to Be Clean, Always

Ever since I can remember, every morning, I'd take the hottest showers. Yet, after the rape, I'd obsessively end every shower with ice-cold water to wake myself up from the nightmares—to snap out of it, I guess you could say. I'd get dressed, go downstairs, and sit in the kitchen's breakfast nook staring outside the big window in our small kitchen when living in Europe. My mind would always wander while my fingers aggressively tapped the table without my knowledge—until Mom would walk in and demand I stop. I was making her nervous. (I was fucking nervous.)

According to her: I needed a professional. I needed love and understanding. Walking on eggshells my whole life was like the tremors after a decent Cali earthquake. In fact, I carried these behaviors to school. I'd tap my fingers on my desk, getting sent to the principal's office for almost anything after my rape. Before, I was chatty and tardy, a little bit of a smart-ass. It was enough for my fifth grade teacher to pull me outside and ask me, "Did anything happen or change at home? Are you OK?"

The questions were painful coming from a teacher over my own family. To be pushed aside hurts.

Being told the truth isn't really so or not as bad as it seems. An absolutely shattering and incomprehensible experience for anyone.

As a child, I was left utterly confused and searching for safe places for decades. My nervousness exposed itself before there was a socially accepted word to dedicate to something still trivial, taboo, even seen as a weakness—even, possibly to this day. I talked openly about my feelings and was shunned.

My obsession with being clean became intense, or I would feel disgusting. Then came the food issues. I never ate to fullness. I preferred emptiness or somewhere in between. Most things were no longer exciting anymore. My brother and I would play outside for hours before my rape. We would make up stories and hunt them down. Our imaginations were wild, and we were free. Now only dancing kept me feeling free.

Today as a mother, I know that, if someone touched my child wrong, there would be plenty of time for something to happen to the sick fuck before 9-1-1 got there. I knew this after holding my first baby. Actually, having my children solidified the truth of my abuse.

Always believe your children. Listen to their details. No ten-year-old would know the things I did. I was told to stay quiet and left alone. I was alone then—with no resources to help me understand.

Today you have so many resources, I know it's still hard. Most importantly, confirming your suspicions. Answering some questions and affirming your fear. Give "it" a name. Especially today, with all the information and resources. Today you can scroll and scroll for the place that's calling you. Early 90's, twitch no internet and no groups to help me understand. No specialized fields dedicated to sexual abuse. No trauma counseling to be able to tell the truth and not hold it in, not overcome my trauma made me hard to understand, not available or too much so. If those few only knew it wouldn't have lasted. I'm more of a homie. But two men got the sexuality out of me no one else ever had. I was fearful and closed off, until these two musicians I met so young, both in ky life for a decade one and decades the other. Knew them both without fame and money and with. Now both more than once. That and working together at studios or on tour made us closer. But thisI speak of is the past.

I will start fresh and pray for the same opportunities, as God does give back what the lotus stole.

I am believing more than ever.

Not love, work and fulfillment.

Just peeking in knowing I am won't give in,
However, your lyrical mind begins to sing lyrics
That lead you to the address and not stress.

Because one knows, there is nothing none when I am home, not a bother or pressed for time. Busy too, especially where I will be working and studio times.

Regardless if you are like me and love and loss seem one in the same: Don't give up on yourself.

You are valid, and you matter. You're not a coward. You're a survivor. Whether sexual abuse, bullying, illness, neglect, domestic abuse, a car crash, a loss of a loved one, these are all traumas.
Anything that leaves lasting pain, leaves you feeling alone, less than, or not enough is a trauma.
You have purpose. Kindness gets us through all anger.
We are righteously deserving of your anger.
Don't hold on to it.
But you are stronger. No Matter what caused it. Until you face it and laugh with that person again. It can eat away. If they say no or nothing. You tried, onward and upwards. WORD?

CHAPTER 18

Hollywood Says, Touch Your Nose

I never start anything without an end today. Why did this book take so many years to write? My full story has many beginnings, and forty won't be the end of the beginning.

Having a new start is like your kiss first.

Only as we grow, we are most in love when God recognizes our heart and brushes our cheek with a kiss. It feels like acceptance, like destiny being fulfilled, while still working toward a goal—pure bliss.

I've had many blissful moments. Even in my darkest moments, I would wait for sleep.

Soon enough, if I played "Oasis" at all, even one more time, he threatened to bounce. We had a relationship that was special for sure. It lasted during his worst two years I had in Hollywood. And I never cared about paying all the bills and giving him my Escalade as his, while he got his music career back on track.

It was time to go to Italy, to see my daughter. He would stay and live in my "penthouse" Up all the night before, barely making the plane. I get there and my daughter, now three years old runs to me. I stammered, playing the role that usually was naturally, but that drug drained me. I'd made it overseas and out of Hollywood.

I was very serious about being trusted and learning everything about studios.

That night changed everything. After over a year, there he was again, across from me. The deep dark pools of his eyes seemed so pure, looking deep into mine after so long. He finished my thoughts. Still can."

I may have wanted too much too fast? I got frustrated when the world wouldn't stop with me. After all the big rushes, dancing nationally, working in renowned studios.

By age twenty-one, I had been working in" Dose" studios for more than two years straight. To this day I regret messing up my legit standing and respect from

Lethal Dose losing his trust broke me.

All that magic that happened and changed my life. Also like magic, poof was gone.

Before I lost everything: Dance kept me alive

Though it was hard for me to cope. I did. Or as long as I could, without healing or feeling.

It led to me almost losing myself another time. I always caught myself and began again. If I went back with dad and worked in studios. I was safe with my crew and protected.

Dedicated to: The owners of the Custom made cars that filled the studio lot.

Truest to this day. Forgive me my boy behind the metal doors of the studio that trusted me before anybody.

"Chevy Le"

CHAPTER 19

Mother: That Hood

Facts—seeing my first daughter for the first time brought to the forefront of my fragile mind what had been hidden behind a blackout curtain for at least a decade of active amnesia. I hid my brokenness well. I will reveal this. To lie to yourself or others regarding your feelings—we call it boundaries in the therapy world—is only a disservice to yourself. Boundaries are important. Letting my walls down for others or this book is not a pass to have my boundaries disrespected. However, I am aware it will possibly open the door for many to have their opinions. And sadly I've found many who don't like seeing others be free, much less achieve. I have always loved seeing everyone succeed. However, I have always known when I'm happy for others, I'm a happier person. It's not only a no-brainer, it's the way humanity should be. I don't want to sound like I'm perfect and saying do what I do. I do, however, know this way of thinking of others first will help you grow.

Many with perfectly healthy brains don't come to peace with their past and, therefore, others who seem to "have it better." You can have it all. And working for it makes your dream more than worth it. Working for what you want keeps you humble and empathetic to human personal trials we can help each other with by being kind.

CHAPTER 20

Tortilla Chips and Dramatical Self Sabotage

For so many years, I was preyed on; those who preyed on me were like vultures sensing death. A girl died that night, but not the strong or even vulnerable one. Many of us believe we are badasses—we're so "strong," surviving it all. Was life always bad? No, my friends. Nothing in life lasts forever—the bad or the good. There is always a change coming. Press on. You can't imagine what is waiting for you.

I always envied birds because they could soar anywhere the wind took them and shit on whoever. Seriously, like a superpower, they could go anywhere. Beautiful thoughts and amazing experiences don't heal you; they're just distractions. Trauma inside chips away, until finally the movie keeps playing and playing. All these thoughts were raging in my head.

Still, here I was cleaning up the damned tortilla chips my-two-year-old son poured on the floor. Then with glee, my toddler stomped on them while giggling—so perfect. Yet, that is the moment Mommy was realizing her whole life had been hijacked. Sure, I was annoyed that there were chips all over the floor. I told myself, from that moment on, my kids won't be haunted by anything, even me showing my frustration. I'm not a saint, and mothering isn't a contest. If you choose love and teach them kindness, you've got this. Jameson started singing the cleanup song—all parents know it—breaking my thoughts up. I begin to sing along, while wondering, How will I write a book? That part of my brain that was obsessing wanted to break free and tell the world and myself it was going to be OK.

I could try not to hear the whispers that, though quiet, had still reached my soul—seeds of doubt. "Still telling yourself no one's going to listen?" I asked myself.

So, how do I write a book? I just start in my heart.

OK, Brooklin, but after you clean up the chips.

The first person I texted about this book was "him." He said, "Sweet."

Then I sent my "him" a speck of a chapter too, written that day. At this point, we'd had a period of no communication in a few years. "He" was who I wanted to ask? "He" texted back immediately, and thus, we began trying again for the next ten months. "He" started checking my stories on Instagram, so I FaceTimed "him" and asked," What are you doing, making sure I'm still me?" "He" laughed. We talked face-to-face for over an hour.

The next person I told was my ex-Husband, who was still processing that we weren't together anymore; that parallel has been hard for me. He said out loud, "That's great." (sarcastically) My Ex was, however, the worst at lying, and an about shit zi woukdnt even care about.

Example: "Bruh, Did you seriously go eat donuts again? You are nearly cancer free. Colon Cancer I might add. Look I know it messed with his Pro-Athlete ego to get cancer at all. He has changed for it someone I used to know since. He isn't all about Life, he is fucking mad at it and kissed "his" body, how dare his body daily him. "Brooklin, your two ex.s took drugs until there fifties and here I am Chrsistmas Eve during he a damn a damn pandemic getting twenty feet of my small intestines remonded. He was, however, amused with my idea to patent that way of weight loss!m? I mean what family do we know that mat just trying anything. He wasn't home until a few days after New Year. I cook, wrap gifts, stuff stockings, make special calls to Santa know my kids are listening, ("So they would take a second to sort their life out/. That is my favorite part. Actually it my kids suddenljng eyed in the morning when they see the Jesus is everyday, so I do love using Santa as a manipulation tool for once in a year. I swear kids are smarter than we ever gave them credit for clean and burn cookies like a good Momma, but I have to say his family life was definitely more built around the meaning and the traditions my moms pink and silver tree we couldn't touch aver reorest with his mind. I knew what he was thinking. *Let's see if she finishes*—or, rather, he would have thought, *if she starts*. But I was smarter than that. My ex-Husband's bright vvathletes state of mind is all strategy.

I had already written enough to secure a meeting with publishing companies and a literary agent. My ex-husband had always been there physically, but I was somewhere else emotionally.

I told "him" first because he is an artist himself and would understand what I was getting myself into. I had seen "him" work on one song for days or longer. "Are you ready for that?" "he" asked.

I said, "Babe, I have to."

"He" said, "Then do it."

"He" left me nine months in. The healing was intense, as I said at the beginning.

There is nothing to forgive, as long as he lives. He was kind to me more than he was cruel. "He" has let go so I could finish this book and get my life back. Will we connect ever again? I don't know? There has been a shift in my life. My age scared him. So did my choices. My trauma and survival made him see me differently. I wasn't the innocent young dancer who knew everyone. I was now forty, honest, and shunned by most of our crew. Most voted for me incognito to win Maxim Cover Girl 2023 at age forty, though. They left kind notes, making a similar point: "It's your time," "Full circle," or "Proud of you."

Chapter 21

Random Feelings Pop in

That feeling, along with being a professional dancer, gave me back pieces of me, stolen that night. To those who wondered why I popped back in like the old days, though life had moved on, know this—I missed you and those days. Forgive me for putting such responsibilities on you all. I didn't realize I was so small to you, because, back then, dancer #2, right behind you, Fred, I felt larger than life for a place I earned and thought nervous most night, your kindness calmed me. I had made a dream of my own come true—after already being more than one statistic. I was raped, neglected, and abused. I became pregnant in my teens, but there were two things at play behind it all—God's plan and my determination. I put it all into dance, mostly. I was so unhappy unless I was dancing or being loved. Then I was whole. This was also true around creating in the studio; on stage watching history being made on tour; and, of course, with my dad.

What about my children? They are a part of me. I wake up crying without my kids if we are apart. However, I also knew I was more than your mommy. I am your role model, and you have to see that the same universe I want you to succeed in wants that for me/us too. The pain I am overcoming must be overcome. Many times, I've failed. I eventually became a junkie. They called me functioning; no soulless human is functional. I almost lost my soul to dope from running away from pain. That's the only reason I'm typing this aimlessly so you don't make this deadly mistake.

However, in this memoir, my memories running into each other aren't even confused after spending decades hiding in the deepest part of me, as well as well documented journals I wrote aimlessly all the time. The way I write is different, as my professor said. But he also told me, "You *are* a writer, without a doubt. One day, you will let it out. Don't give up."

I ended up dropping out of creative writing, getting frustrated with my stories and fiction always being overtaken by one of the characters still being a part of my life. I had to get it out. Well that's cool, because out of my four publishable options, the memoir is what was wanted. It always led to a place I didn't want to go in my mind. There was no ending, until I had enough healing.

I have lost people in my life just over any success. *A magazine cover in my 40's* especially. Envy is seriously such a waste of time. Truly. There is enough room for everyone at the table. Many don't want you to succeed if it means they can't have or take your place. You would think I'd trust no one or become promiscuous after sexual abuse and being treated so nasty. I didn't. My best friend, Lee Christine, will tell you, I am the opposite.

I am too trusting. I've only been with a few men. And I've never had a one-night stand. I had a few encounters in Hollywood that made me nervous.

My dad held his annual birthday party until he turned fifty five at one of our favorite hang outs Rainbow, with Hudson, Stevie and Erik as well as his sober party as Avalon. I can't name them all.

He only meddled in a few of my affairs, my safety, keeping me from using drugs as well as he could, and making sure no more trauma was done to me if he could help it. I still made bad choices, and he loved me through it.

SMORGASBORD: Just extra drizzle from then

This chapter should be called smorgasbord, as my life has always been wildly unpredictable. Until the last two years in real suburbia and I couldn't take it. So I had to make a choice. My ex. Turned into a really bad place for me to think I spent so many years trying for my kids, and my having to be free and making him "shun" me in moments with absolute disgust I have not felt since my rape. Sadly it was so surprising I was physically ill and my faith faltered, until I realized that Satan sent distractions and thought God gave me my babies to make sure I would survive the covert passive treatment. I don't know how I missed all the red flags.

Even so I had to get this book done, it was my ticket out, yet each day starts with me cleaning up after my kids, also ends their day with me doing the same. The whole day my mind's eye ticks like a clock—anxiously waiting until I can sit quietly and get all my thoughts out. I'm aware many won't read everything; skim through, finding the chapters that suit you. Like shopping? Who goes in every store? Fuck who actually shops anywhere, but online anymore? (good thing, my website is seriously out of this world) merch, a trailer, direct book sales to make it convenient, about me, Siri ect contact, weekly lives, and panels for specific needs and ways to get in touch for trauma coaching, tarot therapy, listening therapy and notes I take, along with my personal notes and options for self recovery, as well as the ne on on identifying what I hear and see. You get it and make your choice and have an individual mapped out healing and acceptance leading to outcomes and most of all giving you choices. Choices are a must in healing. There is now one way. Individuality is the best permanent mark we make on this earth. Use it well. You didn't for years. Am I now? I feel I am headed in the right way. Not afraid to expose myself, I made some changes. No longer living in fiction, I woke up and said, "NO!" Knowing I would pay dearly.

My story doesn't make me special. It hopefully makes you see yourself in parts of my many lives. We all get lost and try this or that. Sone him or her. Or lists of both. It's ok. Discover what is and isn't you, one day you will have to choose. I am hoping to make it hard.

I suppose I thought the same about the company as he thought of me writing a book. When and how long? Will you really actually do it?

"Yes, I will," I told him out loud, the day his face shared his doubt.

He looked shocked and then laughed. I still remember that day last November. All I was thinking was, *Will it make sense?*

This book should be called, *ADD, Enriched*. Don't blink or you'll miss how she got where she is. Or is it where she got?

Y'all, just know, I am aware I write like a bat out of a cave. But that's how I feel, except the blindfold is off. The lights are on, and I see it all—the good, the bad, the ugly, and the uglier. Thank God no random guy came to mind. What does still come, but fleetingly, are those demon eyes I didn't recognize on a man I had known most of my life. He always made me uncomfortable. But from age three to that August of my tenth year, I couldn't put my finger on it. And then it was too late. That's why we have to shed light on this epidemic happening right now—without giving too much away. This isn't meant to hurt anyone, but it isn't a lullaby either. I am aware ties will be severed by opening wounds or, as my mother says, "still harping on that old shit."

What if she had simply scooped me up and held me, had never left me? What if she'd yelled at him, rather than pretending all was well? What if she had chosen not to give me a crutch of mental anguish, knowing full well I wasn't mentally ill? I was traumatized and anxious, which was to be expected.

Every psychologist said the same thing about having PTSD from my sexual trauma, which she wouldn't accept. He luckily stepped in and said, "This is only Brooklin's first week in treatment after two full years using both recreational and prescription pills. She will, of course, exhibit "episodes" of all types for at least ninety days.

I wasn't willing to air out my dirty laundry, yet. I am here now airing out my entire closet. Colorful, I would say. Hard to keep up. Not sure which chapter is what.

Nor do I know know anyone who writes methodically. It isn't possible, is it? How can you literally pull out each memory right on time and stay right there with it, until the credits. Are you kidding me? I can barely watch a movie all the way through.

Paparazzi: When it really started-

When we were young and hiding from the paparazzi anymore, he didn't need the attention. He even drove us around in an outdated

Lexus as a decoy. Back then, we stayed in the house for weeks at a time. His assistant grabbed what we needed and he loved my cooking and me sleeping behind him on his studio couch. He had a studio in the house on the hill. That was his happy place too, the studio. I had so many warnings about him back when I was the youngest in every room. There have since been so many years, so many lives, both separate and apart. That's when my heart stopped beating until I caught a new breath.

When I need a new state of mind, I inhale—manifesting what I don't want when I start breathing again. Sometimes it works. This particular time, it did for two months. I was indifferent, completely disgusted to see what level he'd stooped to. Even if it made him happy somewhere in his soullessness of late to see me care or hurt. *What's the difference, when you have been part of the problem for a quarter of a century?* I realized as I breathed him out.

For some reason, last year, we went deeper emotionally again. When we were together, something was off, and now I know why. When one person is living completely authentically, literally swimming in the truth, and the other is still in la-la land, only friendship is possible. He wanted more and judged me harshly for being uncomfortable. I felt the lies and realizations. That was why I wasn't who I had been. I was older, different in my choices. This book brought up so much, and I was hard to control. I am going to delete half of this shit. It's pointless.

Fuck is my favorite word and all I say every morning if I don't fucking type this up. My memories are burning; my head hurts if I don't get this, my stomach is growling; and, worse, I'm ignoring the friction that may come if anyone takes my perception in and wrong. Out of context is Hollywood's problem. Judgment next. Not much different from what none of us should engage in.

Look in the mirror and know your memories are not fiction. You aren't living in digital like this world hopes—dulling pain, preventing healing. Vegging becomes missing it all—free for all. Someone will tell your story a million different ways, but it is yours. Don't be afraid to keep typing. Even one or two words could grab someone's soul and remind them it's time to walk, leap, choose.

I'm no longer living in a ball, even in satin sheets, quietly coming to the sound of your screams to appease. No more pretending. Come loudly. Tell the truth with conviction. What if you don't understand the comparison? Wait until you have to pretend to come or you are too insecure and suppress your ecstasy. Both make me wanna smash mirrors to this day. I wasted so much time not being me. This title is obvious.

I figured it out. I believed in *me*. Boring? Stay with me. I'm doing this on will. I'll blow this wide open by telling your story.

Yet, still I'm a mama. Those damn tortilla chips won't clean themselves up. Like my truth, they're still on the floor.

"You will never be fulfilled until you do whatever it is you are obsessively thinking about."

I began writing this book the day tortilla chips wouldn't move themselves. It takes many times to finally know it's now or never, nothing could stop me—unless I allow my insecurities to lock me back up. If my ambition fades, my fear could take hold. No. I was getting old.

It's now or never, and I have proof for the one person who will show up, calling me every name in the book. She'll come with no valid reason, except, "She's lying." Get in line, Mother. Haters will be.

Yes, that will always affect me.

Here we are. Or it's me, thinking of you all.

Especially while that record is playing in my head. I'm sweeping up tortilla chips with my son; his smile makes me melt. Now my son is my everything. He's everything I prayed for, though his ginger blond hair was a shock. Genetics are strange.

I am on a mission. My son will be a good man watching Mommy fight for the respect we all deserve. I look at him, from above my phone, where he lays across me. I have typed this entire book on my phone. I stop typing when his little arm grabs mine, and he says, "No working, Mommy," suddenly determined. Yet he's smiling the same at him, always and forever my baby boy.

I'm writing the book I asked to write. Will I get it right? I don't know. I have to pee. Sorry, but any writer will tell you, "When you are on a streak, you keep going."

Here I am typing with dry eyes and chapped lips because, now, it all makes sense. That doesn't mean I know what I'm doing or how to write a book, but I'm here doing it.

The record still plays (you may know the one I mean): I'm not enough. Will I finally finish something?

However, this time my need for fulfillment outweighed all my fears.

Now I've spent nine months writing and five typing this book. I have changed since I began pouring my pain out. As has my life, so much since then. Life changes so rapidly. Try to take it in stride—not like me, who lives too fast.

CHAPTER 22

Clearly, Freestyling This Shit

So this book will be news to some. It won't be as simple as blocking someone on social media.

My life, for the better part of 1998 through 2005, was dancing on tours or working in the studio. Finding proof from the late '90s and early 2000s hasn't been easy. Fred has been a saving grace—just as kind as he was when he was my boss and then friend. Friends can be fickle in Hollywood. When I began discussing my past publicly without fear. I have my Polaroid albums from tours, movie sets, and days in Heath's basement while he tuned all his guitars meticulously. He was so funny. We could be in his house for a few days and say only a handful of words or have an intellectually driven all-night dialogue. We hated politics. But unlike most men, he wanted to talk about life and things we'd experienced and how those experiences had changed us. What did we learn? He was the first friend I told about my rape. That was exactly why the memories of filming and friendships in a town that saved my life kept my mind busy.

My adrenaline was always pumping when we spoke, which was rarely. And each time, before she hung up, she always said the same thing. (She thought it scared me, but it didn't.) "You know, no one out there gives a shit about you."

Before we get to the redemption God always gives you, the life he gives back (and better than before), let's finish the memory I could and will write methodically. However, I was starting to feel trapped in my journal. I was going by dates or order of pain. Then like a storm, the pain would be followed by a rainbow after the rain. *Predictable*, I told myself.

I am going to freestyle this shit. Memories fold into each other. So do places. And yet many still haven't tucked themselves away too far in my brain to keep me from unleashing the moments then and now. Unfolding a whole memory isn't hard for me. I just don't write methodically. There is nothing wrong with what consumes us, like when you feel your face flushing from frustration. I was feeling like I needed to take a bunch of deep breaths and see what comes out. What's left of me? This was a question I did ask for years.

That night in 1990 came back to me randomly. I told Ang first. She was very angry and gave me strength to be me. She made me look in the mirror and say, "I survived. That makes me a badass." I repeated that for years.

The happy-go-lucky girl was mourned. She was into candles and blood. I was cool with the candles and drugs. I cared little about myself but would do anything for someone else, even if that jeopardized my life.

Finally last year, October 2021, I called my people in LA and said, "It's time. I am ready to write my story." So here I am, writing a bunch of chapters into one piece. I may or may not kick myself later for not writing methodically through so many memories.

I will focus on my days in Hollywood, where I hid in the wild romances and the background of fame.

There comes a day when many walk away. Let it go. I type this statement more times than I will count; these were situations that stole the most time from me. For what? Especially, if are grown and aware you are trying to help others with your deepest trauma. You are brave for speaking up. Forget those who walk away like you took their toy or some fantasy—now that you're damaged goods. For the first time, I can describe exactly what I saw in the lioness part of me, and so many can't take it. We have to change that.

I was a young girl, a child then. But now I am grown and still silenced. I know it's horrifying, shocking, something no one wants to hear. I get it, but it happens to small children. Listen to me. I still remember every moment. I still rush through the emotional pain, the physical (I still get a stomach pain briefly), the embarrassment, and the sheer fear in tandem today.

Today, there are resources for everything. The beginning of healing is feeling heard.

Breath. You aren't alone in this world. Many of us have been hurt, and more will be if we don't make noise.

I'll be the misfit. I always was anyway.

CHAPTER 23

Coming Back to America

It was all wanted anyway. America was where my sister was, along with the man I loved at the time and the amazing friends I had made (many of whom still remain). (Sidenote—many of them have hit major fame since then.)

I worked in my dad's office part-time, whenever I was in LA. I traveled a lot. I went between my sister; my high school bestie, Jessamyn, who was in DC, and getting stuck in the Hills with my boyfriend at the time. Also at eighteen, I met the father of my first daughter. I think of the reckoning of it all, the powerlessness. My ex calls him #calmate, his checkmate for life. I suppose I felt safe and would go back for that reason mostly. We have made beautiful, amazing children over the years, but I have done that two with others. I prefer them to remain nameless.

An obsession started when my circle grew—and quickly. These were my people. My crew grew like weeds, and I trusted everyone. Looking back, I see that I was not fucking cautious enough. I believed his stability was real. He bought me a car our third week together. He was the kindest person, and he saw the pain I was in; yet he wouldn't know exactly why for years. Other than my dad Weho, I'd never met anyone so unconditional. However, to this day, I have never been able to fully settle down. Maybe I am just my father's daughter. He and I will co-parent for the wellbeing of our children regardless. It's now a handful of kids and many pregnancies later (from the only three men I will be highlighting, as they were a huge part of my life—one until sixteen years ago and the other until just last month).

But it was my dad's unconditional love that meant most. Little did I know Dave Weiderman was one of the kings of Hollywood and ran much of the game. He is still so humble to this day. That's not exactly how most are introduced to their dad. Like most teenagers, I was a rebel without a cause. I didn't understand the opportunities I was throwing away. (I wouldn't until much later, like today, realizing all I gave up.) However much we kick ourselves, we have to get up, sore bum and all, and breathe in and out. I have a destiny to this day. I will keep going. Don't waste your time being embarrassed when you eat it publicly. It's life. And I can't say enough how tired I am of people being afraid to trip in front of the queen herself. Who fucking cares? I do hope I don't stub my toe though, as I tend to lose my composure more than I do when biting my lip while eating so fast—like my life, so fast.

We must take accountability for our choices, regardless of how hurt we are, trauma included. We should never hurt others. Dad taught me so much. He taught me how to forgive, how to be loved, and how to work hard—none of which I would truly take into account until my mid thirties. He taught me early to be in the right place and that earlier is the right time. So I did as he did. And for years life was amazing, surreal. I was eighteen by now.

Daddy was happy for me, and of course, he already knew them all. He was involved in most of the bands, including the FV tours. He would, years later, induct a handful of the bands from that tour on his RockWalk outside the Sunset GC, his home base for forty-two years. However, before I really knew who Daddy was, besides Hudson or Barker walking into his office randomly, I just watched, listened and learned in that infamous office on Sunset.

Daddy let me learn as an adult. OK, OK, he did give me time-outs, which consisted of not leaving and listening to new artist demos for hours on end. He never left the office before 9:00 p.m. The holidays were the best. He kept the store open for Stevie and would say funny dad jokes. And proof of their trust for each other—to

Stevie, the most famous blind man in Hollywood since Ray Charles, Christmas, "Take a look around."

The reply? "Tell your pops, fuck you," laughing.

He later stole the keys to my dad's Mercedes to do doughnuts in the empty Sunset parking lot. Best punishment I ever had.

Let's go way back to 1996, wheels down at the airport. My sister picked me up. I spent my first night at the Viper Room at age fifteen—not knowing, ten years later, I would be dancing there. That was my first night in Weho,. We lived in Topanga.

Still, Hollywood was when my life changed. Time would go by fast, yet I remember I felt an immediate shift in my life that day I landed at LAX. My hands danced out the window as my sister drove. It was one of my favorite moments in life. I knew I was home—though I'd still go back and forth many times. My sister was trying to find her place in life, and I was still running from mine.

CHAPTER 24

How to Write a Book

How do you write a book? I don't actually fucking know, except just start, friends. What I do know is that you must tell the truth always and show up. These are among the few things my dad tells me daily. However, most importantly, you must always love and believe in yourself.

So, here I am, typing aimlessly sometimes, knowing this is gonna be the beginning of something. Other times, I'm calling my publisher and saying I need a few days. I'm just not feeling it. It's not even writer's block; this is my life. The floodgates opened, and my memories came out in a rush for six months. Then I had to take a self-care break for two months.

Sometimes I rhyme. Other times, my memories are like scattered thoughts on the floor—much like my life—scattered pages thrown across a room, yet still taking flight. I watch, like a naval captain ready to launch into action. However, my thoughts are still aimlessly falling on these pages, these pieces of my life. I keep picking them up, alone over and over again. I love words, minds, and the thoughts we articulate.

You may weep or lose yourself for a while. I got lost in time writing this book. Sometimes after hours of typing, I feel like I'm holding nothing but wasted time. Still, it's a part of my story too, just what it sounds like. No need to write about nothing-filled days. So, here we are healing—an everyday acceptance of what ultimately changes us. Amazingly what comes with acceptance is, eventually, peace. And soon, others who are suffering will notice. They'll want to know how.

You then know your calling. That is what the gift of giving and receiving is about. Stay open and humble as you help others with their truth and love, with your story.

Tapping into my emotions was never hard when I was performing or loving my children or the men I have loved—only three in my whole life. As I write, memories interrupt any knowledge with emotion, a healing mode that's hard access. Pain and sorrow creep up still. Ways of coping trip us up, whether they take the form of addiction, depression, or going back to a relationship you know is not where you belong. I am guilty of them all and more.

Life is made of movements that turn into moments, and you have to know which moment to hold on to until the end. Because what if? I may not know how to write a book according to the preferences of some. Maybe you just prefer other types of writing and mine is not your style. Maybe my life and the depths of my pain are too much for some. The knowledge that we all have traumas and need not compare won't be conveyed to others. That isn't my responsibility. There is peace, though, in not being compared or judged for what you have overcome.

My responsibility is only to be truthful, unafraid, and willing to share dark places. Many are still too afraid to go within themselves. That's living on the outskirts of life. The world is full of lovers, haters, respect, and loyalty and, more so, of absolutely none of the above. We must move past those facts of life and live our own lives. The ones who hurt you, push them out before they drain you from your ifs.

How to do anything isn't written in stone. I must add, to make it easier on yourself, draw an outline of your book. I have found the hardest part is organizing chapters at the end. As a creative person, I write as the memories flow. An outline will help your editing process. The first manuscript is always imperfect. It's more interesting to be imperfect, in my opinion. Think of it as the five outfits you try on every time you go out or feel bloated. We all do, right? Yet, I don't know about you, I end up going backward and choosing the first outfit every time.

Next, God starts shifting the universe he has had planned for you this whole time.

Making choices is how we shift the universe and our personal experiences ourselves. We rarely land on our feet. We get back up. So we can work, as the universe is also at work. You will feel the shift in whatever it is your hands were made to do and your mind too.

Nine and a half months ago, I was obsessed with TikTok and knocking my head against walls, raising my fist to the sky defiantly, and saying, "No." I did it silently though. I wanted no one to know what I already knew was part of my destiny, yet I wasn't ready. I had started and stopped so many books—this book, treatments, and screenplays.

This time, I knew it was real. There was a shift, and sudden events began happening in a row. What happened years earlier had lain dormant. It had been there through my dancing, my traveling, my relationships; it was there through my pregnancies and breastfeeding; and now it was here as I was rounding up this book and with the cover of *Maxim* coming up. I wasn't giving up.

CHAPTER 25

No Need to Run: The Truth Prevails

Running from my past was made easy in Hollywood, and became my true home. The life that was mine was completely different from the neglect and abuse I had known. The good times didn't even compare to this life. I finally forgot, for years, what had happened to me. The nightmares were still present, and some were paralyzing.

The truth prevails. No one deserves to have their *no* taken away. No one deserves not to be heard or believed. To be afraid is not a weakness; it is a protective mechanism. Not everyone will choose to get healing, help others, or how to utter the truth of the moment that stopped our entire world long enough to completely reprogram us.

The sooner we can be honest, if only for ourselves, the sooner we will be freed. The chains of bondage screaming, then eventually you will realize it has affected all of life's beautiful moments, once bright and full of careless laughter. Whittled down over time, everyone is different, and so is every reaction. Know this—there will be a moment when you will realize, I have to let it out. I began screaming in public without being able to get it out yet. I was sixteen the first time this happened.

Today is different. Don't feel defeated in your journey. I'm doing this on will and because too many people have told me, "You'll blow this wide open by telling your story."

Except, right now in my house, as everything seems to be falling apart. Having my independence?

On that note, I know plenty who would love to have thoughts that plague me, like the title implies. This book has been whispered to me quietly for years. Then it got too loud.

I know more than anyone that life changes. But that's become particularly present for me since I hit over forty.

Be prepared for your coffee to get cold. Think of the dinner you didn't eat. Everything has shifted in just a matter of minutes that turn into weeks. I have cried, and I rarely do.

How about writing that book? Do you think it will just be your reflection? By letting it all out, you will undoubtedly relive your most painful moments. I personally chose to write about the most painful memories first. That isn't professional advice, just my choice.

Then there's the scariest part of any endeavor you attempt on your own, alone, with all your heart.

This is my first time aiming to become the published author of a book, without having any guidance. I haven't qualified myself at all. I'm finally doing something many have asked me to do, including those whispers inside me for over twenty years. Timing truly is everything, and when it's your time, you will know. You'll become absolutely determined to make anything happen. You will finally start something that you kept putting off. It will come easily, quickly, and clearly. Friend, that boss inside you looks different than anyone else's. It's the comparisons and untrue things *humans* spread that keep you from moving forward. Believing in yourself is key. And so *is knowing it isn't you they hate, it's themselves.*

How do you write *your* story? Live it, own it, and believe in yourself.

Not like the robot I became at ten, paralyzed by fear.

CHAPTER 26

The Birth of the Bizkitettes

A month before my dancing was focused tediously on training in dance.

I met Robin, known for choreography. I would end up dancing a few years later at the Viper Room, where we had guest stars weekly. The show included many acts and a dance ensemble before five became a group. I was blessed to dance at a few shows where I met Carmen, and we became friends. That led to me being invited to her rehearsal dinner and wedding to Navarro. I haven't spoken to either of them since 2009.

It was the late 90's when I first danced with these amazing choreographers and dancers. I was hoping to get a professional job ASAP, even at only seventeen. I was hip-hop and burlesque almost exclusively. Finally, there was an audition I was ready for and felt good enough to go for. As you may have figured out, I got the job. And I did it on my own, without my dad's "word." It became our Family Values and dad believed and the life of dancing professionally was born. It's just that he wasn't my dad yet—which was how I wanted it for at least a full tour or more. I was a part of the industry in many ways. Brooklin's opinion always mattered to Dave Weiderman. Through his public relations, we were a good team.

Dad taught me to be in the right place earlier than the right time. So I did. I had bounced back from the loss of my pregnancy and the depression that almost took my life through dancing. I was excited and terrified all at the same time. I never followed through on anything because of my fears and insecurities. I was never free again after being raped. Who is? However, my dad was proud of me before I felt comfortable calling him daddy.

Still not quite eighteen, I was deemed an adult.

I remember standing on a stage in front of thousands and realizing I had actually accomplished my dream. My first tour with Limp included a music video on the road.

This is when I should tell you that nothing was glamorous. We didn't have a huge bus like most think. We had a van and slept in it a lot. Which was fine. We were just starting. I loved it. We took showers at arenas or rest stops. It was hard work. However, it was all fun. Fred was hysterical and always had his well-fed bulldog, Bizkit, by his side. He gave me his blessing for this book saying, "It will be good for you."

This is my story. And, yes, my life was wild. Dad was happy for me and knew who they were—of course he did. He was involved in my Family Values and tour was second. Later we inducted a handful of the bands from that tour on his RockWalk. However, before I really knew who Daddy was, I just watched, listened, and learned. It all made sense in the office on the boulevard.

I felt like, up until then, my life hadn't even begun. I went to the Grammys with my dad when he was nominated. This was the same year I had made the cut as a professional dancer. I don't know if any of us knew how much our lives would change. I certainly had no idea it would blow up the way it did.

It wasn't about sleeping in vans—no not the shoes—anymore.

We were basically mini Freds. Some girls got to ride in the tour buses if you dated a band member. I didn't date any—OK, not publicly anyway. We partied on different buses. Usually, I was tired and wanted to sleep or train before the next show. I did have to pinch myself. I had no time to let it sink in. I had no time to take it all in.

Before I left, Dad said not to tell anyone who he was. Why, Brooklin, because, you earned this." "I wanted to be seen as the trained dancer you are"

I loved hanging out with Fred. He was funny and always had the best advice. His bulldog, Bizkit, was his baby and on the bus, always.

Then it would end, and we'd go our separate ways. Then we'd do it again the next tour. I stayed busy. My life was finally beginning.

Chapter 27

Cake, Baked and Burlesque

The year was 2000 (the best).

The Viper Room, formerly the "Melody", was the first place I went to party, at barely fifteen. Then seven years later, I was working there as a chorus girl with the "Dolls."

I'd worked with our choreographer for various auditions. I auditioned for many music videos and live shows.

I had hung out next door at Shamrock, a tattoo shop. Boo Boo did most of my tattoos and his father too. In fact, years before, across the street, still on Sunset Boulevard was Tattoo Mania (which has been gone for years now). That was where Boo Boo first worked and where we originally met through mutual friends, Seth and Spoon. Both were so kind and my first friends in L.A. Then Boo Boo went over to Mark's Shamrock. And of course, I followed. Also, I must give tribute to Boo Boo.

Shamrock has been a hangout for decades. Also, it was just a few blocks from Viper Room, as we called it. Johnny was a co-owner for many years. Many know the stories of "RP" passing. I wasn't around for that. However, Johnny was and did stick around the joint. He was there most nights in the late '90s and early 2000s. He was at most shows. He loved what we brought to the Viper Room. He loved the old days and was super creative, and old-fashioned as Chivalry men are concerned.

I was lucky to be included with Christina and Carmen. I became close to Carmen during those few years.

I attended her rehearsal dinner and wedding to Navarro a year later. Carmen is an absolute gem. She is one of the kindest and most generous women in that wild town.

I was barely nineteen when we originally met, and then we did the "Dolls," at only twenty-two. This was when the paparazzi were just getting crazy. So, I'd sneak her out of various places, most not there anymore. Joseph's, Concorde, Avalon. Where I threw my Dad's 55th birthday. Basically, we would do a show and head to a Bolt or Herman event. She left by 1:00 a.m.

I was a mess and would end up at Guy's on a Sunday when I should have been sleeping. I missed many auditions or was late because I chose poker night on Tuesday at Hyde's until 3:00 am over a 7:00 a.m. call.

I wasn't even playing poker. I was refilling tequila shots. That was Hyde's favorite drink. I opened his freezer as I was cleaning and rearranging one night. It was full of Patron. Hyde was so kind to me, knowing full well I was high as hell. He trusted me to be in his home. I asked once, "Why?"

His response. "Your heart. You don't steal. And all my friends wanna bang you. Lastly, my girl likes you." Our parents were friends. Her parents were in a band in the 60's too.

I rolled my eyes but had to laugh because he was serious as fuck. I also adored B. Being friends with Mark meant Sunday basketball at his house in the Hills. However, if it was during the season, Mark would joke, "You'll suffice, Brooklin. I just hung. I didn't play. Mark is truly kind and may never grow up.—which is what makes him great. Mark wanted to be an NBA player. Do we speak today? Not really.

Time passes fast in those hills.

LIKE TIME PASSES FAST:

I left Hollywood in 2018, planned on coming right back. Life took some twists and turns, again. I had a dream of my then eight-year-old daughter in a white gown reaching for me. I was boarding the last red-eye that night. Three weeks later, My daughter was diagnosed with cancer.

Devastated, the girl who always had fire under my feet, (me) had to stay in one place. Being still only happened in one place. In Hollywood, life still happens. It shredded me worse than fucking Shawn White in the Olymics, yet, here I still am. Telling you the truth. As mixed up as the ingredients of this batter may be, it's cake and it may or may not taste great, but it's life. Most things are not things anyone hasn't had at some level. (You can.)

We all have the ingredients. We just have to accept how our cake comes out and when we bite. Bite for yourself and what you create.

CHAPTER 28

Working in Studios

I had just retired as a professional dancer. I had no plans on moving to the south. It's where my ex. was drafted, his NBA career and then his career-ending injury. I was a new mom. I started dancing pro again—local and one short tours. Carmen headlined at a "Dolls" show. I was dancing the chorus three nights a week at the Viper Room on the Boulevard. It would be a few years before my addiction took over, after dancing professionally since I was seventeen. Now I was twenty-two and working at a studio where a ton of renowned bands were recording. My job was to take care of the place and make sure shit wasn't out of place or stolen. Platinum, Gold, every award and record, I was finally trusted. Then I fucked up, as usual. And with drugs—the one thing Le said you can't touch. So many warned me.

They told me who was dangerous and who to stay away from. Yet, I didn't listen, and I'm still paying for it. Le truly cared, and I fucked it up (like most relationships). However, my best memories come from learning how to run that studio. Of course becoming a mother and attending Strasberg were fulfilling. In fact, Lethal Dose let my daughter, "Raquel", who was two at the time, run around the studio when it was slow. We would color or listen to beats he and Danny mixed. They all adored "Raquel".

She is grown now. Her innocence meant so much to them back then; it's a sweet memory.

But it is just a memory. Skip a bit. During my recovery from addiction, Erik and I sang, "Friend." I sang the chorus. It got me through my first detox from dope.

Is *shame* true? No. But the truth of what feels shameful can be motivation, over a constant bad memory.

CHAPTER 29

Help from Above

I'm doing this on my own, but I know I have help from above. I have been handling my past with kid gloves for too long. I have heard whispers and written them down. It doesn't matter when the whispers began. It took me years to even figure out it was coming from my own heart. I never told anyone because that would sound crazy, right? It took another decade, and the triggering dreams returned. This was before I even knew there was a God, who, in fact, was in my heart. He speaks gently; many don't hear him. Some think the idea is that they are rewarded or punished by a God. There's more. Love and kindness is the main reason I love everything about the spirit circling all of us.

Staying focused and consistent is a bitch. He has to be helping me. My head is pounding, and I keep going. I'm sweaty and full of emotions, yet I keep going.

Then we come to where I am, and I usually fall. But now with help from above, I will see this through. This is gagging some of you. I did when I was told the simplest truth. I just have to love, be kind and keep going? All of us have felt broken from the pain we carry. I would say stop. I am carrying around the pain for someone who doesn't give a shit about me? I ask Spirit, Why? He just squeezes my heart to love more. "He" pops up, nameless for a reason but a huge part of my life. And I'm learning the good, bad, and ugly.

So I will hold it and the memories of the beautiful soul I met many years ago and the way you made me laugh just months ago. I hate that revelation, but the era is gone.

Battling ourselves is the hardest part. Part of that is holding on to pain that isn't ours. It wasn't always pain. It used to be the happiest moments of your life. Most don't care or think you don't. It knows that you're worth every bit of anyone's time you have chosen to give. If they don't see you or your worth, fuck 'em!

You have work to do. And trust me, they were always a part of the plan, whether they know it or not. Destiny is a funny thing. It involves more pain and abandonment than the rainbow at the end or a big win.

Life is a trip. We all take different ones, so writing about what we saw, believe, know, and the detailed memories we perceived is perfectly important for all of you and for others.

It's hard to comprehend friendships or love affairs ending, and abruptly too. It will be a year in October when I lose my first friend to this book. My writing and intensity while working wasn't the Brooklin he knew. In Hollywood, forty is a Pentecostal sin. I may be on the cover of *Maxim* with an eight page spread, but I'm forty.

The rock stars left. The athlete stayed.

I have been pushing away the one person who stayed, even after I said the most awful things. The same way "he" very recently treated me is the way I have been treating my ex for years. I don't mean it. I am frustrated with myself.

This book and *my latest magazine cover and story* are well overdue. If you have a fire in you, know you are gonna burn people with love and pain. It's hard to handle at first for everyone who knows you. The only ones who will get you are the ones you meet because of your fire. You can quit on people too. See if they come back. Life is short. I prefer to be guided by my heart. I told you about two people I lost since this book or turning forty, maybe both. Only one has a spirit kept close to my heart. I have memories of him throwing a ball in a hoodie after he was just on stage in a damn space suit and wild makeup. I recall his intense stares from across any room or studio we were in. I remember everything, down to the pain of losing children for his career. He wasn't a part of many decisions regarding my children or ours. I made my choices, and it may have been the spiritual nail in the coffin for us. I was given three gifts. Many girls get knocked up on purpose, but I wanted him to soar in his career. Do I regret it now? I do 100 percent; it's part of my pain. Our feelings aren't anyone's responsibility—unless they choose. I was given that chance by him over and over again. I ruined it. As far as the friend I loved and thought would always care, he ran as soon as I changed even a little.

That other close friend has recently resurfaced. Just a few months—done. I even threw his hoodie, my favorite one too. I threw it over his balcony last spring without a word or a note.

My ex. helps me raise all my kids. Some of them are his and others I brought home in my belly as his own and never ever makes me feel bad.

But either way, remember the facts. You are in control of where you choose to put your precious energy. If you choose to give it to someone who may not care, that is because the universe is using you still. Energy travels around the earth. Never give up on what your heart tells you.

CHAPTER 30

Why Now?

How did I know it was time to write all of this down? That it was time to share my life and memories for strangers to hopefully or possibly devour? To surely make assumptions and possibly judgments?

This isn't just writing a book. This is letting anyone in. It's dangerous, but not more than children everywhere being abused and feeling alone. Just as important, grown men and women are out there feeling like something is off, missing, or starting to surface.

It may mean nothing to you. And this Brooklin's University of light, love, misery, fear, freedom, and living most of all—finally at forty—may open up the compartmentalized dusty shelves in the back of your brain. It may move hidden memories to your conscious mind. You may have a loud soundtrack you have turned down to hear the truth your spirit is whispering to you.

Some say, "What does it matter? It happened, and you're alive. Move on." You can. It's just so heavy that way.

A whole book—damn, what does that even mean?

CHAPTER 31

Working Mom Shit

My toddler climbed on me. So were my thoughts from my past presently almost raging to get out. It was finally becoming clear to other people and to the most known doctor in the world. I was so angry with Dr. Phil. And so was my new little fan group of over a hundred thousand between each platform since 2017, who had reached out to me. All thanked me or apologized for not watching until the end the first time that shit show aired. Dr. Phil still saved my life.

He triggered me and my family to find change—all but my mother.

Being misunderstood on that stage still led to my opening Pandora's box.

A renowned Doctor back home, wanted us on his show to talk about my ex-husband's NBA career and how that contributed to my drug use. The show played on tv for years.

However, many of those who watched the shit show until the end expressed the same response. "I can't look at your bulldog-faced mom. Has she always looked so mean?"

"Yes," is how I reply with pleasantries, but just like now, I am holding back for so many reasons.

They're not important.

My sister used to say, "And there it is," laughing sarcastically. She did this at her house or at theaters, every time the title of the movie we were watching was scripted into a scene. I always laughed and thought, *Well obviously.* Everything we watch or read is derived from scenes and themes from lives. They also say you're a "real writer" if you have more than one book in you. Oh, I do.

After the effort and stress that goes into what still is a mess of paragraphs, some will stay; others will be gone by tomorrow when I turn this in to my publisher's. I'm constantly needing Advil, as my head throbs, focusing to get this right. The worst is when I've spent hours writing, eyes watering, mind on fire, and my sweet twelve-year-old asks for simple things. She is 87 percent blind since her brain tumor. Yet, fighting back frustration has become harder since I started typing this book out. My thoughts are flowing through my thumbs. My bladder is full and so is my head. I look up in a daze, and there is a tiny figure, saying, "Mama, Mama, *Mom.*"

"I heard you. I'm coming." Then I apologize as I rush to give her what she needs. As she walks away, I'm disgusted with myself, afraid I made her feel the way my mother made me feel.

I ignore my thoughts, knowing that chapter is now lost or will never be the same. I have to stop my daughter. She is halfway up the unvacuumed stairs. *Jesus, Brooklin, why do you have to notice everything? Focus. The life you want for you and your kids doesn't exist without you succeeding* at this and anything from here forward.

However, my children know I love them. I even express why Mommy is consumed. "Mommy is going to make it all up to you," I tell them.

My daughter is my twelve-year-old. She inspires me, as she does everything anyone with two functioning eyes does with less than one. She nods and hugs me. My heart warms and then breaks as I sit and stare at all these thoughts, the unorganized pain and watch my child feel her way down the stairs, not wanting help. *Suck it up, Buttercup. Talk to yourself. Talk in third person or in first person. This is your story—verse by verse.*

There's no bridge. I jump straight in. Maybe I should contemplate? Nope—boring. I searched for the memory I was typing before my daughter needed me. I was focused, and now I feel scattered, even scared. Then I look back up the now-empty staircase. She is safe. That's what matters. I weather through a headache and force myself to ignore my obsessive desire to vacuum, as I did almost daily before I only typed this book. My ass is numb, and my mind, exhausted. I refuse to stop. My biggest fear is confusing you. Please keep up. This story is rough-and-tumble. But we will not stay in the weeds for long.

I have been writing all my life—to escape. I have poems, screenplays, short stories, tons of other ideas and half-written "projects" stowed away.

I've lost too many who I believed were "safe" places at the time. Wasted time is what those tumbles were. Watch who you let in your life.

Yes, all these things and more are racing through my mind—like flying saucers, pictures, and buttons, like on a jukebox. If pushed, it will open a whole new memory—which is constantly happening.

My apologies. I can tell you for sure I still feel lost in moments. Even after standing in a fifth of guilt for rushing my daughter, afraid I would forget my train of thought, which isn't hard or her fault. I had at least four stories race through my mind while walking back to my desk, bed, or leaning against the kitchen counter typing away, startled by little voices all day.

I finally chose to seclude myself in my room for six hours a day until this was done at the nine-month mark. As a mother, I know that nine months means it's time to give birth.

I told myself to stop whining. If I can make this book come together and it works out, my kids will understand. If no one else will, they will.

CHAPTER 32

My Mind's Own Time Zones

Now redirecting my thoughts again, I bought myself more of my mind's time zones. Before I got burnt out, I had to take the six steps back to my phone. I tried not to count them, but it was six steps, with a pivot and quick turn.

Then I ran up the stairs and quietly made another quick turn down the hall, hoping my son was still napping, like he was when I crept away for food less than twenty minutes ago.

Quietly, I counted the fourteen steps to my bed. I tripped, stubbing my elbows, as I am the klutziest. So for the fourth time in twenty-four hours I cringe again in pain. Usually, I cuss like an asshole, scream and moan like I have been shot, so I've been told. Either way, the motherfucker hurt. And I whispered, "Fucking, fuck, fuck," as I gently creased the covers with my still numb ass. Was this bed flattening my ass? *There I go again. Just sit, Brooklin. You are your racing thoughts.* So much to tell you, too little time.

They say few things happen in less than a second. Wrong. I lost most of myself in less than five at ten. Are you ready for more? First, I was thinking of all the turns I'd missed, the ones that made me late, cutting my first impression in half. I thought of all the little and the big choices we make in life. (Blah, blah. Should I hit delete?) Yelp me.

I left this chapter here, where I left half my typed story. I started to prop my pillows. Before I could get comfy, my son woke up.

"Jesus, really?" And then I felt my bladder burning. Fuck! TMI. So, now I was beyond frustrated. It was no one's fault; it's life.

I didn't have the luxury of going away for a month. Nor would I ever leave my baby son—said the woman who will finally have to get this done. I cried daily for their future and my freedom. I breathed in deeply for you out there and me. We need freedom.

I was, however, yearning, burning to pour into these pages all the stages I went through as a result of trauma. I also wanted to tell you the many things we who have suffered trauma go through, so anyone who reads this won't feel alone. Many houses are made of glass. Many are filled with evil scheming, so the empire doesn't shatter, as a result of the sick secrets getting out.

I suddenly became frantic. Now it had been twenty odd minutes—changing Jameson's diaper, mommy peeing, and washing our hands. I wasn't rushing his life for mine—which isn't easy for me. Many will agree. I got him a snack and watched him in a gooey daze. I witnessed the love I had for him, my hope for his one day. I wished it were me starting over, but it wasn't. We began again.

Again, that's OK. It looked different; we may too. It was as it should be. Even if my ass is flat when this is done, it shall be done.

Finally, I set my son up like a king. He was so cute, using his baby pillow as a recliner now. Fuck, where did the time go? He was growing too fast. And then my anxiety began to do the same. Time felt like the enemy more than anything or anyone. I got so distracted by anything and everything, especially my children all day—whether it was them driving me crazy or me watching them, bursting with love and gratitude. Then I'd snap out of it, and my other obsession would buzz. And I knew it was a text war I was praying for.

That is the end of that chapter for the day.

Did I get anywhere?

"Maybe Tomorrow," is a mantra we have to let go of. Today: or now or never. (Is how I think)

CHAPTER 33

Ends Lead to New Beginnings, Always

Two days ago, I made the cover of Maxim Magazine at forty-one. Never stop my friends. Not my first, but we shall see, I am forty? Wait ladies, that doesn't matter. That same day, my stepfather fell over and passed in less than a second. My whole life has been this way. Extreme is the best way to put it. Losing my stepdad has impacted me greatly. I am so grateful my Father is still alive. However, he was an amazing man and I lost two siblings I loved dearly. Poppi is what we called him, he would never allow this decision if he was still alive. He really kept this side of my family together. My Father worries more about me now.

What does that mean? Me, gutted, yet always overanalyzing.

You aren't damaged; you are destined.

I realized I was afraid to fail. As I begged myself not to quit, my son jumped on my lap, landing on my bladder. "Fucking really?" I did say it out loud, like "one more thing." But not my baby, his cuddles are like breathing for me. I could lie and say I thought it or whispered it so the child wouldn't hear. Nope. That is not what any of us are doing here—we're not here for lies and fairy tales. There are moments that are fairy tales and moments of pure hell. Nothing lasts. As depressing as that can sound, remember the hell won't either. I wish I had everyone who will read this book in a room. I would love to see the expressions, the Karens grabbing their heart, probably worried my son will be scared or an asshole. He will survive the many times he'll go through those moments, as his mother is furthest from "A Karen." He will not be afraid to do it, even apologize for being a jerk.

Oh, chill. He has already said *fuck*. What am I gonna do? Stop? No. I never cuss at my children. Nor do I yell out "bad words"—wait, unless I stub my toe or elbow. That shit pisses me off.

I hope some Karens read this. No offense. Fucking let your hair down. Maybe take your bra off. Or here's a thought—how about refraining from judging anyone at all?

On that note, this book was predestined for me to write. There were years of whispers, first quietly and then louder. Then finally I began. Even going home to Noho, the wrong ball started rolling. I got distracted for months. Now, my son gets his own snacks. But here we are back again.

Look, I don't know how this will play out. I just type it out—on my phone to start, and then I format it. It's the hardest job thus far, especially because, like the title, I don't know how to write a book. I just type when my brain is on fire. I can tell you I'm afraid to fail—so much so, peeing is a fucking luxury. I have over fifty journals I wrote in during my stints in rehabs. I haven't opened or referenced one. God said, "It's all in your head." So I type until my eyes are dry; my lips are chapped; and I'm definitely dehydrated, though my bladder is screaming. My coffee is cold, along with the dinner I didn't eat. Everything has shifted in just a matter of months. I have cried and done many things I rarely do in years—except, let go. I just began to do that. It's the hardest part and the last lost puzzle piece you step on unexpectedly. Yet, you know exactly where it doesn't go. So put it back—and not on the floor where you could carry it all over again on the bottom of your shoe.

CHAPTER 34

Stepford Wife Moments—Argh

He was drafted into the NBA and crazy about me. It was like a scene from *Stepford Wives*. Suddenly, the house had pictures of me, and my mom was cheerful, proud I was with an NBA player. But I skipped the four years most moms would be proud of. I wasn't conventional, but I made my own way as a dancer, working in publicity and full-time in a renowned music studio.

Just a little less than four years earlier my Mother wasn't speaking to me, nor knew where I was. A few weeks before turning fifteen, I started my period at school. I called my mother that time too. And she said, "I don't believe you. Go to the nurse to deal with it. And you'd better hope this is real. She paused. I thought she was going to realize I was crying. Oh, she did. Her next words? "Dry it up." Click.

When I tell you I found a way to get somewhere else fast, I mean it. I was on a plane to the United States. My life would suddenly be on fast-forward, and I would be in an alternate universe.

CHAPTER 35

My Gap Years

This is about the many times I left Hollywood. As my home base that is. I left primarily to be in what I thought would be more stable for a child. Apples in oranges, I tell you. I was pregnant again and wanted a healthy baby. I am extremely loyal and will always forgive. Of course, I learned most things the hard way and would be lying if I said I wasn't hurt many times.

I had a healthy baby girl. My ex. Husband Cal Bowdler was playing in the NBA. I had to go back to Hollywood in 2009 and again off and on to get away again from his extreme control. He controlled me through my children. I had to come to him to see them, and I would break every time and was flying every six weeks and still trying to pay bills. I had help from friends and my dad out there. He made sure I worked and earned it. Which was one of the best lessons he ever taught me. That and to always be honest, lies turn into catastrophic messes. If I grew up being told to lie about what and where people were in the house all the time. I hated it and always felt it was wrong. Now one of my daughters is having similar behavior after staying with my mother since my step father died. It terrifies me for my kids not to be honest and able to ask for forgiveness without their ego getting in the way. Lies also keep people hiding things, not caring who they hurt to keep secrets that aren't there to keep. My book was days from coming out and my ex. served me with paperwork for custody after refusing to let me take my son to see his sick grandpa.

I have primary custody as the mother and we are unmarried. I have never seen him willing to purger himself until… I am for the first time feeling like I have been in the same life as a complete stranger for 23 years. I left so often because his behavior was obsessive and controlling.

Sadly I've had to age the last ten years because my children mean everything to me and he stopped letting me take them on trips. He let me do things when I was using, but now seven years clean I can't have any freedom or my own financial freedom. I am finding out the lengths people will go to to hurt someone to keep control. It is so hard for someone like myself, who has spent so much time in therapy, had healthy brain scans and reports, to still talk to someone while myself talking to audiences through different guest spots on podcasts about overcoming trauma, staying kind, trying not to dwell on the blame game. However, telling your story is important and someone does need to take accountability. If they don't like it in my case, you have to be brave and realize you are worthy and your abuser and those who cover for them are not well. Instead choose to affirm yourself and your constant willingness to get through another day, until you are able to not only think about it, but do it fearlessly. This book has been hard to write, because the nightmares and flashbacks are constant again, but I shake them off and move forward today. Being emerged in the depths of my still sore soul reaching for the moments that I realized need to be acknowledged. Why? Because this is not a pretty subject, it's the most disgusting of life altering events to happen to a child. I wrote this book reluctantly at first, however, now as I run through a book that was supposed to be published. I have decided it is best that you know. This is happening right in your neighborhoods and kids in your school. It is rising at an astounding rate and researchers are attributing this to the desensitization of today's society.

Most will heal best and most comfortable away from the abusive environment. Just remember wherever you go, you're still there. This is not a pity party either.

Today visual of the aftermath being raped resembles the Swiss waterfalls in April, flowing down the Alps fast and furiously, on a mission. It's beautiful and strong and knows where it is going. We are stronger than we think.

Make a picture of what your life and trauma will look like from now on and tell yourself to go there every time the flashbacks, nightmares, or anything that plagues you.

It's a start. Journaling helped me as well.

I am finally on a mission. I hope I can execute this book to the end. I pray I am able to draw a clear picture with my words, as clear as hundreds of Swiss waterfalls, somehow missing the tiny mountain road below. I drove them many times from Germany to Italy and always thought, *Those waterfalls are fast and on their way nowhere fast.* They never made it to the road, yet they were absolutely hypnotizing. Though methodic, they were wild too. *Wanting to be a waterfall? Really, Brooklin? Snap out of it.*

Those falls have been flowing for decades, like the epidemic of sexual abuse. There was, of course, the silence of the pain. Now I hear the rushing water, and nothing will stop me. You are as beautiful as those waterfalls. To this day I daydream and have nightmares. Had I known it wasn't my fault, this story and me becoming every statistic wouldn't have happened so horrifically. No one let me express my pain. I often think, had the truth been acknowledged in any way, I wouldn't have been tortured all these years.

Now, as a mother, I want to be clear that a person wouldn't be walking free, much less walking with a limp leg and dick—sick fuck—if he were to hurt my child. My mother's neglect is something I don't know if I will ever understand. I am no Mother Teresa myself. However, try me when it comes to my kids of all things. I already feel misunderstood, and I'll be damned if my kids don't feel safe in who they are and expressing themselves. I read them books like "*Unfuck Yourself*" over princess bullshit. I pass on Cinderella being kind to the mice, good night. As for Mufasa dying in *The Lion King*, now there's a story I will read over and over again. To be or not to be? Be noble and kind. Fight for others and be authentic to yourself is the truth.

In my nightmares, I still wake up angry. I hear in a strong tone, "Don't be a cry baby"—the words heard her say for so, so many years. To this day, it makes me livid. In truth, I couldn't stop crying, I just had no one there. I remember fearing the worst, her walking in as I cried about her leaving me alone that night. Her choice still puzzles me today, but it no longer haunts me. That night, I was left alone. I finally, slowly got out of the torture chamber of that floral-covered bed, experiencing sharp pains I'd never felt before. The pain shot up my belly button. How was a child supposed to process this?

Today, there are resources. And more people realize this is an epidemic and that those who speak of their abuse must be believed. However, you have to come forward despite those who may try to frighten you. Then, I was met with horror when I cried. As a child, I was told, "It's only as bad as you make it." Years later, it would become I was lying or I was mentally ill. It felt like an attempt to drill those mistruths into my head. A ten-year-old's pain was ignored—when her mind was still young, still barely developed. Suddenly, nothing made sense. Somehow, I knew I wasn't me anymore. I didn't want to be seen or swim with my cousins like I had the day before.

The one thing I never stopped was dance. It kept me out of the house and gave me a six-year professional career by my late teens. However, that night at ten, I wanted to cry. I wanted to cry forever. But why? Thank God, if I would have, none of my dreams would have come true. And continually, I was a fighter, but this changed my whole strategy. I had to plan everything. I no longer knew who to trust. No longer was this a safe place. Nowhere was for at least five more years.

I know this, friends, there's a God. Hold on. I too felt like everyone knew. My confusion was indescribable. The next morning, terrified, I finally opened the locked door out of fear. I walked down the long, dark hallway afraid, searching for what? I didn't know. They say before "it," I was like a bubbly brook. I didn't know who I was anymore. I know. Who does at ten? But isn't that the best thing? The freedom of childhood.

I'd lost that throughout the hours before—from the moment the assault began to when I was left alone in the fetal position. Finally in the dark silence, once it was clear no one was coming back, I pulled back that ugly, heavy floral comforter away, praying it was a bad dream (even still). It was those drops of blood and the pain that confirmed the reality. There was no other explanation for them. Sitting there in the oversized white T-shirt I was still wearing, I looked again, squinting and touching three red spots. *Oh my God, that's blood.* Weeping, I let out a shriek. Then scared, I stopped, instead experiencing my deepest, most confusing pain silently. I was in so much pain, and now my bladder ached.

The visual then came back full force. It still does to this day. I close my eyes, shake my head, and look away. For years, I reached for pills and dope. Not yet; I was still a child (though had they been offered, I didn't take that escape yet). It would be me, myself, and lifelike memories for years. That night, I was staring at posters on the wall, wishing I was them, while he told me this might hurt, treating me like I was an adult. I was a child.

I was afraid to leave the room. I sat there realizing I had to make a choice. I tried not to think of the horrors and the physical pain. The mental anguish thus far was endless, shaking. And still when I remember, a chill crawls up my back.

I wanted to cry all the next day—or forever—letting anyone who looked see the shame and my mother's lack of love. But her scorn kept me quiet.

Now there are resources. There weren't when I was ten, before the internet. Back then, I switched my tune by the next morning. I could use this as a power play over my mom—that was if my mom was still my mom. She was ruthless and selfish. I was no Angel after what happened to me, but I was mostly afraid and unsure. It was her motto and mine as a traumatized ten-year-old. It became a part of me for the next handful years. Then I got out and started a new life.

To all the moms out there who want to be your children's lions, as you should, I believe in you. *Please,* believe your children. That will be 60 percent of their healing and block out future torment.

Rape is a strong word, but it should be heard. I have accepted my mother, after years of manipulation and guilt-tripping. The truth is, she's still in denial. By age thirteen, when I finally began to turn pain into hard work, my life began to change. For a good ten years,

Thigh Highs and No Lies

I compartmentalize my life. Like putting a book on a shelf, I put the abuse I had endured aside. I focused on dancing, and that victory will be told. Your dreams can still come true.

She started to realize I was about to bust, and soon. I was a teen and pregnant. She had to get rid of me. Finally, when I was fifteen years old, she sent me away. The trauma would rearing its ugly head for years, on and on. I would use substances to numb myself. However, I didn't talk about what happened to me for thirteen years. During that time, I used my pain for gain and accomplished four of my dreams and tried all of them, except this one. I didn't let it stop me.

I did need to get away from her. That is a separate book.

For a year, I still trained in dance. Sitting in my dad's office, I met all the musicians my sister had on her walls as a teenager. I learned a lot by hanging out at my dad's office, going through demo's. Again, keep reading and you will see where that led me.

I guess, I needed a big dose of rape to get away and meet my dad and be a little badass, as my Dad still calls me.

I never let anything stop me.

By seventeen, I was on a stage in front of thousands of people on the most popular music tour of the late 1990s and early 2000s."

People hold shame and blame differently. But today, as a mother. I can't fathom not choosing to protect my child, instead hushing and seemingly resenting my own child. The choice I made was to make my mother pay—which wasn't my best choice in life. I was barely eleven, and I was hurt and angry.

This did, however, change everything. It finally got me out of that place and my life.

Yet, I am still the one he chose to ruin.

I look back now and I think, *Dude, I was only ten years old.* Then my memories go back to soaked sheets and my long, dark hair stuck to half my face from the tears and his sweat. As my mom finally approached, I slowly turned my head. I can honestly tell you my fearful thoughts at that very moment. *Am I lost? You're here.*

Then comes my next memory. She wasn't there for me. She was there for herself.

As a mother now, the forgiveness, or lack thereof, eats me up at times. I think of my mother not choosing to hold me, to help me, instead leaving me alone in a room in the back of a big unfamiliar house and never coming back. Skip forward five years of hell, in my anger, I was sent to my older sister. Hollywood changed my life. Things happen in life.

Hold on because you never know what God is about to send you. Go with it if your God gut is calm—if your tummy is happy and your mind is clear.

Pain has a way of making you stronger and more empathetic, though you'll be afraid at first. We who have endured pain love hard because we don't want anyone hurt like we have been. My friends, don't spend too much time angry like I did, choosing to be relentlessly kind. Your vindication is coming. Choose to believe you deserve to be wined and dined. All you have been through, trauma is all the same—pain and shame. But *babies*, you are strong AF and wise.

Tell yourself this—*those who hurt me are sick, and it's not my fault.*

My mother has been afraid I would write this book for years. My mother—the woman who I called Mama—is practically a stranger and has been.

I wish I knew what exactly to say. But I know this, you are so worthy. The cold sweats and glimpses from the past will never fully stop, but numbing them with drugs doesn't stop them either.

Are we done here? I hate staying in this place too long. Let's move to what healed trauma turns into.

CHAPTER 36

Hollywood Back Then

Glam? Many ask? Surely most wonder?

Depends. Love kept happening in the midst of flashing bulbs.

Everyone wants to know about the glamorous stuff. What was it like? Well, first, touring isn't glamorous. It was fun as hell. And as Limp became more famous, showers in the arena and sleeping in vans became four to six girls in a hotel room. I never minded. I wanted that life. I worked hard for it—so much so no one knew Dave Weiderman was my dad. And that was how I wanted it. I wanted to earn my way.

I already knew some of the boys who were on what would become an epic tour.

My relationship with another band's lead singer, many may think my choices of older men have to do with my trauma, but I certainly was aware of my participation. Even then, I stayed in a model apartment when I tried to get to get along with her. Living with my mother has always been unhealthy—not just for me but also for any of my siblings.

It was during that get away that I met my ex. He had recently been drafted into the NBA. We met at a place called Karma, also owned by my former agent. Christina Aguilera had just thrown up on my shoe, and the DJ dragged me to this big dude in a dark corner talking to Dennis. So I thought, *OK, big brother is trying to set me up?*

It was the DJ who was doing so, and neither he nor I ever saw him again?

He played in the NBA, in Italy, and as an Irish citizen with Ireland's national team. I spent much of my time in Los Angeles working, as well as carrying on my on-again-off-again affair with music and a musician. For four more years, I danced, as well as attending plenty of auditions and, later, rehabs.

However, before my addiction to drugs, came my first addiction. It was love. I won't say men, because I can count on less than two hands how many I have been with. In fact, the same two have taken over twenty years of my life. I love few. However, I love hard. And surely it came off as more than I really felt. I am always concerned for those I care for.

I will tell you a few stories.

This book has put me in a time warp. I see the truth now, and I wasted time believing we were cool, no matter what.

CHAPTER 37

The Last Days of Rock

However, let's talk about the last days of rock, for me. Family Values was the beginning of a huge chunk of my life. If you ever saw the show, you'll know that, soon after "he" would exit stage left, we Bizkitettes would run on from stage right, directly after his band performed. So if you were a Family Values fan, maybe you can guess who opened for Limp for three years. Once we were done with our set—which was exhausting and, apart from Korn ending the tours, was a good hour of wild intensity—I was on a constant high. This memory is still part of the after-show routine. After he is done with his set, he plays with something. Now it's him racing through buses on a scooter—which makes me laugh and annoys me at the same time. When he is on tour to this day and we are near each other, I go and meet him. I still get butterflies. He made fun of me for calling him *buddy* last week—because we are more. One part of me wants to keep it light. The other? What does he want? Who knows?

Let's get back to the '90s, when I was young. We had worked hard. Though many think I was always there, I wasn't. I auditioned at "MDance", which is still there and trained at Steevy recently. Of course, today, having a paid partnership on Instagram is what proves who you are. So,

In the late '90s, before all this shit overcame real life—before selfies were "selfies" and just "Kodak Moments." Back when camera phones didn't exist—I had a Polaroid camera. I took pictures of every moment on every set, every party. And of course, it was stolen. It only angers me now. I would love to add a picture for every memory. I had some and what I do have shows plenty of memories.

Did I ever believe twenty-five years later I would still care? Never. Neither of us did, actually. This past trip, I, unfortunately wasn't myself. I was stressed, not able to relax. He could tell I still was consumed by something. Unfortunately, he thought it was him. That, it wasn't. My assistant was flying to Hollywood and would be there in hours. I was so different, grown, and finally professional. It had been five years since we'd last rekindled our affair. We were so passionate. This last time, I wasn't all there. I was overwhelmed by everything and trying to focus on him.

As of last week, he made it clear he would never love me again, and our connection was gone forever. He also said, "Focus on your book, Brooklin. We are so unhealthy and obsessive." We did have this crazy connection. We laughed, could talk about anything, and never worried about trust. I miss that, and his silly texts or random FaceTimes. However, he is correct. I have to focus.

CHAPTER 38

Clearly, My Favorite Days: Let Me Count the Ways

By the age of twenty-one, I was working fully in music studios. That night, we hadn't seen each other in two years.

Still, we snuck out the back before the first course. That's how we have always been in a room. We can't be that close to each other without the tension sweeping us away. Then we would end up ditching life for weeks, huddled up at my place or his. At this point, the house we spent the next month in was my favorite of all the places we loved as long as he could.

That night, before we could go to San Marco, I had to check the studio and make sure all the equipment was turned off and the tables were cleaned up—normal management stuff. I had a key, and "he" was shocked.

"You've been busy the last two years," he remarked proudly.

"Always," I replied slyly.

Just like that, we always intrigued each other.

Hollywood is different, but back then, the world was less messy and smaller. this was particularly true in Hollywood. So this affair happened before my first Family Values Tour. We told no one and pretended we didn't know each other. Interestingly, I have never been jealous or wondered what he was doing or who he was with. I relished when we were together. Maybe it was being around music since

I was a kid, in studios with Dad and in Hollywood, itself a different breed. Maybe I am just not the jealous type. In fact, "he" is the only man who has taken up so much of my time. He's the only one whose texts or calls made me smile for the whole day. Admittedly since starting this book in December before the pandemic.

My daughter was diagnosed with cancer, I disappeared for five years. Then I just popped back up when she was cancer free, and I wanted that life back. I was working and living in Hollywood, in wardrobe on a Netflix set.

However, I had a dream that my then eight-year-old daughter was reaching for me and woke up in a cold sweat. I was used to working for a few weeks and then going back to the South, where my ex was still working closely with the NBA and a tech hip-hop company, "The Rap Plug."

Currently working on producing movies, as well as serving as the chairman of the Film Society. So moving home wasn't "ever" feasibl.

I never want to separate my kids.

So my communication with my past has been very important. I let a lot go by, never again. Your dreams matter and so does your WORTH IN THE MAKING. Why him/them? You can.

I need to be clear. Fame is an illusion. I see Fred as Fred, him as him, JD as JD. "Pennington" was one of few old friends who never ever felt comfortable with fame. He was, rather, the opposite. I miss him too. This book has pictures of me on his set at eighteen. When you leave that town for too long, many will forget who you were to them—or what you know about them.

I know many want me to tell secrets. I do know many.

CHAPTER 39

Third Person and Beautiful Vampires

Years kept passing. My life looked charmed on the outside. I was lucky, true. I promise you, none of that matters, not if you feel like you're living a lie. I couldn't hide from myself. Only life always moves on, from the outside.

As I type, my two-year-old son is sprawled across me, watching a YouTube learning show. He's so relaxed, without any worries. He has his own iPad at two. I know. What's the world come to? All the while, my TV is also blaring, a Netflix crime drama in the background. Forensics has always interested me. Still, obsessively, I type my story, trying to place each puzzle piece where it belongs. I work meticulously, feeling guilty every time I have to stop, even to be a momma. Which is ridiculous. Life never stops, not for anyone—certainly not for filling blank pages, turning them into full ones. Putting each part where it belongs is the hardest part for me. Where does anything belong? Of course there's a timeline, and an exact one. However, when you spend most of your life suspended between one experience and the next, separating what you remember clearly, into full scenes, not pieces, can be tricky. Then there's the fact that time brings fear to many, although it's an inevitable part of life, aging.

Time is a daily cage we have to work ourselves in and out of.

We're emotional contortionists. Many never feel trapped, or do we all feel caged? Then freedom should bring relief, right? For me, like with most things, I felt disappointment, even rage. In the end, I was never free at all. Even once I finally accepted what happened and knew deep inside it wasn't a death sentence, I still lived half alive most of my life. Honestly, I wonder if anyone could tell. Living to make others laugh, falling in love young and too fast, and those other behaviors directly related to being a broken human being, broken by another human—did anyone notice? My heart was broken, but I refused to be beaten.

That's called trauma. Or is it the walking dead? Beautiful vampires afraid of nothing, and everything at the same time? Sunlight blinds and then kills the pain you lived with all your life. Or mine?

Tell me yours. I am realizing I write in third person randomly, still not to feel the pain.

CHAPTER 40

Puzzles Pieces Need a Home

I chose to finally type this all out—not from journals I spent thirty years pouring into, even then holding back.

Facts—my handwriting is too messy anyway. Still, I write memory after memory, few of them in order. Organizing this book for my publisher is going to be a bitch. I am missing yet another family dinner to focus on you, yes you, book. You are that which consumes my mind, my soul, and absolutely my body at times. All these thoughts inside my head.

If you have questions, let me know on my website. Direct communication.

I encourage deep breathing as you remember.
I forget myself. Don't forget yourself.
However, it helps you sort out things you may not know had a noose around your neck and heart. take deeper breaths as you may feel pain. I am breathing in and out with you. If you want a different picture than "Ang" as Lara Croft or in *Mortal Kombat*, picture me, sitting alone, leaning against a satin pillow, hoping my long, dark extensions are happy and wondering if I will ever finish this book. Deep breath—that was doubt and trauma trying to psyche me out.

Suddenly, picture what love is. Quick transition? Well, let's dive in, or I will never fit the essentials of life up until now.

Love hurts and heals. I have never had trouble loving. I have had trouble being loved. The greatest gift is love, and the most painful is to be unloved. Being vulnerable is a brave way to live life. At least that's what I tell myself as I get hurt; the most has been while writing this book.

I've always been able to access any moment in my life, like a movie. It's more like a drive-in than a theater. It would be in order, by employing you to come and see how the popcorn tastes. The words are popping in my brain and settling down in a bowl I call my mind. They're puzzle pieces that need a home. I still need fresh air as I breathe them in. Similar to Redbox, my recollections fall down a corridor, my deep memory space. Others are triggered. Those I've had to learn to tame. Like a trigger, keep that safety on, and take deep breaths.

CHAPTER 41

Addiction: When Did It Begin?

It began beforeI knew it. Before I knew it, I was addicted. It wasn't just drugs. I was addicted to love. I fell in love three times in my whole life. I played it cool with two. Maybe it was the drugs or his eyes. Or maybe, just maybe, he treated me like his special girl. I now know it wasn't healthy. In fact, we spoke yesterday. He hates me this week. He does that. I have had to let go of a lot to write this book. How freaked out Hollywood gets when an insider writes about the inside. I will tell you there were wild parties on Olympic, and I lived off Sunset and also by Hollywood sign on Beechwood. Then I lived on San Marco off of Cahuenga. And my perfect view of Hollywood sign was off "Whitley" and "Franklin."

The earliest 2000's, when we bought the penthouse—twelfth floor. I could see it all. I could see my past, and I knew my future. I would have two beginning and endings high above Hollywood, the Hollywood sign in full view from my large painting windows. It was a little too ballsy for someone terrified of heights. I would sit in the windowsill at night, waiting for all my crew to get ready at my place for an easy walk to the boulevard. I knew they were passing by and looking up, knowing I was getting ready to go to Joseph's, Beauty Bar, Concord. And Chateau was a drive, but it was a nice hangout.

To now be forty—still loved, but not fought for. You see, Hollywood is like the trauma that happens to many squared. It throws us out no matter who we are or who we're related to when our time seems to be up. My time isn't up.

To those in the hills in those mansions overlooking the mayhem, they did overcome. *Yet*, now they won't leave their homes—which are full of pills, contracts, and assistants taking piss tests because insurance get so high after the *Hustle* and *flow*.

I wish I'd paid more attention to producing. However, I was too busy trying to learn not so awe important Hollywood practices. Like who is a groupie and who isn't? (Lame) That was my job description at one point in a studio I worked in.

Trauma is scientifically proven to cause symptoms confused with mental health Issues. I don't have anything other than PTSD. The anger, the neglect, the hurt, and your trauma with a capital *T* are valid with a capital *V*. So, what next? We make like Spartacus and fight. You're worth it.

We unfuck ourselves and never forget we choose "unfucking" will mean something in our lives. Being and getting fucked are two different things.

How will you walk into a room from now on?

CHAPTER 42

Fucked?

This world can make us feel fucked. However, I don't want you to miss out on all the beautiful memories to be made. Trauma and shame steal from us, time mostly—time believing we are not OK. You are going to be OK. You are OK. We think life is fucked. Let me tell you, it can and will be many times over. It's up to us to talk. It's up to us to be the survivors we are, to *unfuck*, the world with empowerment, and to fuck up those who turned their backs. Now that is where I really want to change mindsets. No more blaming. Life happens, and our response matters. We are strong. And blaming gets us nowhere.

Even still, enjoy life. And make new memories. We do have to let go of the painful ones. It's easier said than done, I know.

Chapter 43

Violated and Villains

Will my story scare people? It already has, but it isn't my whole story. Nor am I the only child who has been and is being and will be violated, yesterday, today, and still tomorrow. So what are we going to do? Yes, people, you? What are we going to do while so much innocence is stolen? Stolen from children, including me?

What are we going to say when the circle comes back around? One thing I am sick happening under our sun is senseless acts of violence against children, as well as many others. But it's the young ones that make my stomach curl and my memories swirl. This is one thing I'm prepared to fight for. This is an epidemic; we need an army.

It's the one epidemic that leads to almost every pandemic out there. Why have I chosen to speak out? Fuck, a regurgitating prophecy: Blood isn't thicker than water. Love is love. And as my dad says, "It is all we need."

We need kindness too. What would you do if you knew the child next door was being abused? Keep quiet?

Chapter 44

Not Wanted: A Theme

One of my first memories of being abused was when I was seven—sadly by my mom. It was quarters being thrown through the dining room and her not caring I had been hurt. My elbow, head, and even neck were injured, after a regular argument between her and one of my older siblings.

It was a foreshadowing of the neglect that would consume my life. My sister filled in always, until she got older and lived her life. She is almost eleven years older. That experience was too much for a seven-year-old. I daydreamed a lot to forget. My sister had always taken care of me anyway. However, as she got older, I became more scared she would leave, like my oldest brother had. My sister was the one to bring me forgotten things to school and to take me places. She changed my diapers when I was little. I wasn't wanted and told often by my mother I wasn't supposed to happen.

Thank God I not only know God now, but my dad also made sure to begin instilling positivity in me as soon as he finally had me. It was too late for some things, as I was already a teen by then. However, it is never hopeless and would ring true later, when I was ready to believe the beauty he saw in me. While I felt devoured, destroyed, and like trash, most saw my heart. Back then I was straight up searching for love and acceptance.

Today, not so much, I prefer mutual respect and no more expectiins. That has changed my life the last five month. Take hatebseriously is eriously our own fault.

If someone is a dick, don't suck it anymore, even to remind them what there little judgment day for a dumbass groupie has seriously cost. Umm one authenticity. Oh not let he clear. We attract narcissists and do they care. Yes, when? Idk? Why? Idk? Is it worth it?

The make up sex after sone dumb shot and a few funny text and break, he'll yeah, but I am different now than my 20's.

I wouldn't recommend that,; it will come. Be patient, or most relationships will undoubtedly be ruined—and for nothing but your lack of self-awareness. It isn't a character flaw, though it's seen as a flaw and not attractive in a society that wants us not to feel. Yet, we do. Those of us who suffered trauma are too eager, and other times we're without any feeling at all. We can flip-flop easily. Some get to us, and I will never know why.

When I was a child and young teen, it was my sister who brought me lunch money and signed school papers. Skip ahead a few years, and it was my sister who brought me clothes after I started my period in Ms. Haley's social studies class, because my mom wouldn't. When she finally had to leave for college, two years later than she normally would have, my sister settled in Los Angeles. She always sent for me, yet I bounced around my childhood seems mostly of memory's if trying to hold inij sobs daily from my moms outburst'sI was cold and scared, my arms were scraped, and I'd skinned my wrist and face and had hit my head hard on the icy broken concrete. Even then, I knew to pretend to be OK. However, she just dropped me off at pre-K without ever asking if I was OK or hugging me.

This is a common theme and not one I want to continually dwell on. However, we have to understand that abuse comes in many different forms. Who categorized it all anyway? Society? The individual is the true story. The survivors will only survive when their pain doesn't label them.

My stomach pain would only worsen over the years. It's commonplace for anxiety to rear its ugly head in those who've experienced trauma.

We moved to Germany when I was young. Yes, children are resilient, as they say. However, children are fragile, and children aren't only sponges. Children are moldable clay. It is *our* job to be there regardless.

As a mother now of a handful of children and three girls at that, I'm keenly aware that pain and trauma can happen in many ways. It will be deepened if it isn't respected with belief and support. We have to stop comparing and assuming. No one deserves to be violated in any way.

This truth usually makes anyone I tell my story to angry or, worse, without words.

Speak out. It happens. And if someone trusts you, value their trust, their story, and them. We don't need a fucking medal. However, disregarding humanity at all is horrifying.

CHAPTER 45

My First Business "Move" on my own...
(Flashback)

Next move—I became chill with Lethal Dose and showed up at his studio in flip-flops, a white hippie dress, wet hair, and sunglasses, just days after dancing on a tour.

I had to get to the job I had come for. I showed up on a warm November day.

I found the big building that Erik mentioned to me. saying, "If you don't find it, ya don't."

By the way, Erik is not someone to bullshit with. He sees through everything. Once, I was following Erik to his Valley home, and he motioned for me to pull over, proceeded to get out of his car, and calmly walked to my window. He motioned for me to roll my window down. Erik told me calmly and clearly, "Slow your ass down. This ain't no race. This is life. There are rules."

That has stuck with me as much as my dad telling me to never snitch. "Do the crime, get caught, do the time." *Yup*! That became sound fucking advice in my life.

I might have slowed the speed of the brand-new Caddy CTS that night. But slowing me down is practically impossible in life. Even still, my brain gets exhausted from *not* accomplishing something. This book is a bitch, no joke. But I finish what I start.

Thigh Highs and No Lies

I'll get to how I have learned to take it down a few notches. I'm told I can be exhausting. I have big ideas and get excited. Don't we all want to be understood? Yes, but we can't make people get it. Take that day at Lethal Dose's. Erik had given me the address just once, and that was it. I was to find it and never ask again. I found it a day later. I was nervous. I'd always wanted to work in music and studios like my dad—before I even knew he was my dad. Life always leads somewhere, and where it does is all yours if you go for it.

It was a bright fall afternoon—breezy. My hair was in my face. Maybe that was why he ushered me in so quickly. These Are the perfect days in Hollywood, eighty degrees tops, nice and breezy, is the best. In general, the best climate I have ever lived in was in the Hills, for sure. The studio parking lot gate was up. Not for me. I could see by the look on his face he was surprised to see me at the door. After he had opened the huge metal door heavy fucking, three-inch-thick, soundproof metal door. It was across from Hollywood. Off a Boulevard, and I could hear the loud noise of the highway, only an exit away. Lethal Dose is always kind. Come to find out there were cameras everywhere, so he probably saw me sitting in my Escalade rehearsing what I was gonna say. I had three cars back then. I don't know why I thought my Escalade was "studio worthy?" He opened the door quickly.

I immediately forgot my spiel and said, "I'm gonna work for you."

He barely paused, smiled, and replied, "Can I get your name?"

My response? "Oh, you don't know me."

Lethal, a DJ we all know and with at my shows with Limp. The biggest tour I danced on, smiled and muttered, "I know your face. It will come to me." He knew my face for sure. However, I wanted this job on my own.

He then said, "Your dress is see-through. Get inside."

(First, off I didn't know that, and yes, I was quite embarrassed.) (White after Labor Day doesn't count in this warm year around town.)

I was yet again in a place I knew would change my life. This has been happening a lot lately. But this shit, daymmm. I was lost in a sea of plush red couches and guitars, the sound booth straight ahead. And to my left was a see-through room with an L-shaped separated glass engulfed room with full mixers and keys. I saw a back room (the groupie room, I would later figure out.)

I got used to them on tour. It's a part of that life, especially the older they get, but they're over it just as fast.

Anyway, back to scanning my next move and the job I was gonna get. I saw phones, which I could answer to set up studio times, interviews, or shows. Lethal Dose was always playing or producing—that or souping up his old Chevrolets. He was in his studio everyday by 3pm.

He smiled, and I had the job and began working that day.

He gave me cash sometimes, but I never asked for a rate. I didn't need it. This was an opportunity for me. Lethal Dose tried to change my life many times, but I was still sick over one man, who wasn't his favorite person. And then by year two, it was my addiction making me sick. However, I had a solid two years running Lethal Dose's studio, and I worked with my dad as well. Lethal Dose was good to me. As you will read, there came a point where no one was really left—especially since writing this book.

However, this is my life, and I am happy to share the good and the bad. Take those risks; you never know, and rejection isn't the worst thing. It is the universe keeping you on track. I wish someone had told me that back in the day.

I started "work" that day. I answered phones, checked the cameras, and got the few who Le did let in that ridiculously heavy door in for their studio time. He laughed at me the first time I let someone in. It took me at least four huge shoves (damn door). Other times, I wasn't able to answer the door. I quickly figured out who to open the door for and when and which knocks to ignore. Lethal Dose was particular, I still wonder how I got in.

Fatal Mistake: This would be my end…

It was a Sunday night at a place called "." I had never seen so many freedoms and celebrity in one place.

But this night, I was sitting outside getting mistaken for "Natalie Imbruglia" who I never knew. I was talked to by uninteresting people who other girls were panting over. I sat alone, as the cover band, "Spazmatics," played. Scanning the crowd silently, I made an inventory of how weird this town really was. I still love it today, though. But no doubt it's weird AF. Seemingly out of nowhere, a large figure appeared. I looked up, unphased. We locked eyes, his as blue as mine, and that tingle I've only felt a few times in my life ran through me. Then he sat next to me, silently.

A few minutes went by, and he was saying out loud what I was thinking. "That's a groupie. They used to be hot. Never act like that." Next, he was saying something about a popular '90s grunge band whose lead singer was five four at most. "He's short" and on and on... I started laughing. So did he. He went on, "but he's a musician, so he'll get the girls." I was soon laughing out loud.

Then Danny asked me, "Did you come alone?"

He told me not to drive alone again. (I thought it was cute. I needed to be put in line sometimes. I was careless and too fearless to him.)

"My friends were inside, and I needed a break," I replied.

He remarked almost too quickly, "Don't drive down here by yourself. It's not safe." (It was another red flag I didn't see; again I liked it.)

We people watched and mumbled silly ideas about their lives or the hangovers they'd have the next day. He told me it had been nice having me around the studio. He walked me to my car around midnight after over an hour of bantering back and forth, speaking the same language.

I had been working at Lethal Dose's for at least three or more months at this point. Danny was there every day. The sexual tension had started the first month. He loved making fun of me like a schoolboy. That night, however, was what made us inseparable off and on for the next two years. Then we both sorta came back and forth.

I had the key to the studio by the first month and brought three pretty girlfriends sometimes if Lethal Dose was in a good mood, but no guys were allowed. Many would follow us after a night out, but they were never allowed in. Even the paparazzi caught Danny and I getting in one of my cars that I let him drive early in our relationship. He was in control; there was no doubt. I knew he liked to be in control, so I allowed it. We would go out for a little while and talk shit and make fun of ourselves for wasting time. Let's be honest. Over two and a half years, my drug use had escalated. Therefore, I was sometimes a perpetual knocker who didn't get let in. (Just being real, I got real fucked up and was punished. However, Lethal Dose and Erik both tried to get me clean and detoxed at different times over the years.)

Nevertheless, for the two years, things ran smoothly, and my oldest daughter was at the studio during daylight hours. It was awesome. Unfortunately, at some point at the end of year two, I tried hard dope. It had been hidden from me for so long. Me becoming unhinged broke his heart. But he had a business. He gave me a chance, not knowing the risks. Trauma unhealed is a risk. It isn't a question on a resume though. So where to we go.

We get healed my friends.

By now, I was working part-time at GC with my dad and was also still at Le Dose studio. My disappearing with "him" was putting me on serious thin *ice.*

I made a few "sick" calls about me or my daughter. I would do that with "him." I'd lose track of time, that's for sure. I always hoped this time would be different.

Now, eighteen years later, as I write this after a traumatic year of communication and still seeing "him" which wasn't the same, I don't know what happened. Was it this book? Was it my age now, or how I'd apparently forgotten how to kiss him, as he said? I could no longer run my fingers through his hair. It was gooped up when it used to be fluffy. We used to be so passionate, breathing into each other instead of coming up for air. This time, it was awkward. Too much time had passed because of the pandemic and other factors. My first everything felt like my last anything when he didn't come back three days later and when my assistant left, like he promised. Then he said there was nothing left—like I was just sex. It gutted me. But he wasn't the man I knew anymore. He was judgmental and stressed, though still loving in person. He wanted more than communication.

He asked me to move back. And when I said, I couldn't, he pouted for a minute and has been mean ever since.

Our story ended, and I thought it never would. Nor had it ever truly begun. None of them knew me, had no idea who I was. I didn't know me either.

But that's life. I savored moments.

Probably, like this chapter, I'm all intertwined. And thoughts drop as I remember vividly all the moments I mattered and all the ones I know I didn't.

"The past, those years in this chapter and this book, meant something. They have shaped me and my children. This is my life to this day you will read—a wild life. There is a whole chapter on tours, my dad, and inducting rock stars to RockWalk on Sunset.

Hollywood and the hill I love, this chapter is a lot. However, it's one of the biggest parts of my life—and in the lives of all my children, except my gorgeous son Jameson, who my ex and I had three years ago. We made him during the hardest time of my life, between my daughter's cancer and the pandemic. He has brought so much joy and healing related to the son I'd wanted to raise at sixteen. There were no teen moms back then. It was taboo and terribly hard. It felt like the red-light district behind closed doors sometimes, but I thought it was love. Be careful with love. It's fleeting.

All the Polaroids I took were stolen, and the rest were ruined during the one flood I was ever in. This was before selfies and social media; this was before taking pictures with friends who were famous was not weird before social media. It was fun; it was growing up and smiling. It was a time of being quickly being forgiven. I was forgiven a lot. I did seem to push the limit with most. I didn't mean to. I am always searching for the truth in others.

How did I get there or here or anywhere?

I met someone who saw me and I didn't see myself. If I had, I wouldn't have messed it up.

This was way before social media. I was fighting for my place, and the outcome was in the lead singer's hands back then. I should have focused on what I'd stopped running from just ten years ago, but I got stuck in my best moments—the moments that finally gave me purpose. Before, it was so strange. People, I had the most surreal moments, even passionate ones, forming lifelong memories. I'm always moving forward in my mind. If I grit my teeth, it was true and kind. Getting older is not the cougar town everyone says it is.

Chapter 46

What and Biggie Smalls?

Biggie and I were tight in the loneliness of my room. Many ask who helped me get through back then besides my sister. Though not anymore, for years, which felt like a lifetime, I felt trapped. I saved those journals, thinking one day, if I did write a book, I'd need them to access the memories that tormented me over the years. I haven't used even one journal entry. My memory is still too clear. That pain doesn't just go away. So, we must let it out at all costs. What do we have to lose? It's all in my head anyway. It wouldn't leave even as I begged. And Lord did I, many times over the years.

When I chose to finally type this all out, I didn't rely on journals I'd spent thirty years pouring int (which also kept me overwhelmed, I might add). I was always holding back because of all that typing—that and, many times, scribbling in my messy handwriting.

Maybe I know I only have a certain amount of me to give.

Our greatest gift is love, and the most painful experience is to be unloved. Being vulnerable is a brave way to live. At least that's what I tell myself as I get hurt or write this book. I've always been able to access any moment in my life, like a movie. It's more like a drive-in than a theater. I need fresh air as I breathe the memories in, most of them. Similar to Redbox, my recollections fall down a corridor, my deep memory space. Others are triggered. Those I've had to learn to tame.

CHAPTER 47

Love Your Hopes and Dreams

Maybe I should high-five myself for just being here. Because the truth is, not everyone will like this book. When it's real life and all, it's messes. I was a chameleon. I could fit in anywhere.

Authenticity is the maker of all things that end in truth. However, humanity should come first. Trying to play off my forward statements, everyone is somebody. No one is nobody. So I say, *no* with a few *rights*.

I finished writing this, as I lay in bed.

Jameson woke again.

Motherhood calls.

So does life.

Love,

Your hopes and dreams

CHAPTER 48

The Truth: That's All

I wanted too much too fast. I would get frustrated after the big rushes of tours. It felt like the world had stopped. Clearly it didn't. I did.

Today, I have to dig deep to remember that girl who knocked on Le's studio. It was tucked away, off a highway across from Hollywood Boulevard. I remember that look on his face. He was stunned to say the least.

I still don't know why he let me in. Maybe I was a bit determined at twenty-one. My energy meant business. I was the same twenty years later, fighting alongside my daughter for her life while she had brain cancer. We're all able to overcome fears, even after severe trauma. However, what about the in between moments in life? We want to always be lions, right?

While sitting up in bed listening to Mel Robbins hoping to get hyped up, I realize writing a book is draining. Even after I was let down by her answers on a podcast, I see she is wise and real. Humility is key. It was just her lack of humility that taught me the importance truly (I hope). Robbins made it clear by answering a question with, and I quote, "Now that you're not a normal person anymore." My jaw dropped, and I prayed she would correct the podcaster. I know they can say what they want and be happy—truthful or not. She didn't. This, in turn, made my jaw drop.

There I was at home with a sick child, struggling to get this done, losing my train of thought.

Just know, everything in life that goes up *must* come down—making room for what's next. Don't take it personal. Enjoy your achievements and hard work—wherever they take you or however far. Hard work lasts longer. I am not knocking social media. I have fun. There is a difference between this life and "real life." But the world is changing. To some, telling the truth and being kind are the most valuable virtues in our daily life. Not that it wasn't always like that. This is what I make sure to instill in my children.

Though my intentions were honest and I was open, sometimes being too open is a turn-off. This was way before I knew how imperative it was to be self-aware. Nor did I then understand the importance of the ability to read any room I was in.

Everything I would need to know in life was right in front of me, yet I wasn't ready.

First and foremost, being self-aware will change all your relationships for the positive. Did I make another U-turn? Y'all that is my life. A bunch of crazy shit has happened. And I am trying to organize it all. I'm going on my fourth trip home to Hollywood to write. I am most inspired there, as that is where I truly became me. The moment I landed at LAX in 1996 at age fifteen, I knew this was my home. As I let my hands fly out in the wind to the music, yet freely on their own, I said out loud to my sister, "This is home."

My life would become one most would dream of. However, enjoying it and cherishing each moment were not always a part of my daily "ritual" I reused to go with the time ticks and a days thst end. You know always if gravity. I just lived. This is why I am so adamant about telling you to be prepared for the seasons of life.

My friends, part of your daily health should be to completely and totally cherish yourself, humanity and respect you, regardless of the past. Second chances after major fuck upas time passes and amends are made. I was in until I was 24 and that is when I feel apart. Until I get home, on my own.

Know that you do have a place in this world, even after severe trauma, addiction, depression, or anything that has held you back. It will dissipate over time. While working at the most coveted studios for years and with my dad, who ran public relations for bands and musicians and founded the RockWalk on Sunset, I skipped around and used what I was taught by my mother—and that was my looks and not my mind. Dad had to unlearn me. When I did use my mind at the table or help musicians with lyrics, strategy, and even advice, I remember their surprise that I wasn't just a pretty face. For three years, I watched all this magic happen in these studios and meetings with Dad, being asked who to sign or induct the best musicians onto the RockWalk.

In the meantime, I was also filming music videos or grabbing tour dates as a dancer. I even got the role of a lifetime after five weeks of audition hell. This was when real acting was still a thing. You started in a room with a few hundred at times more, all of whom looked alike.

CHAPTER 49

Let's Never Compare Ourselves

I remember Dad telling me, "whatever others see is their damn problem and projection. Baby girl, no negative thinking. My Dad is about truth and only truth, never be unkind, and don't snitch. Do the crime, do that time. For serious, he was proud of me for doing thirty-days for charges caught by association. I knew they would be stopped, however, clearly my ass meed yo be sat the fuck down. And it has helped me in life. I remember the day that advice actually clicked.

We all know what we want in life. But you do know what you deserve? Remember, you are no less. Please, look at yourself and say, "I am fucking awesome." No really. Right now. Say, "*I am fucking awesome! I am going to do awesome! I will be kind to myself and others!*

OK, so I just said that out loud with you and realized how upset I still get with myself—that I didn't know the power of my own words until my late thirties.

You have a seat at any table you want. *Own it*! We affect others by choosing kindness and willingness to take the backseat no matter who we are. I never was one who called shotgun, but damn, I was irritated when I was sitting in the back. It was so backward then. Now, I could care less.

Let's get back to 2002, after Le let me in his studio and, in less than ten minutes, agreed to give me a chance to help run his studio (I had my own key in less than a month). I did that job well for my usual two to three functional years. That's how I functioned back then. No one taught me the fundamentals. I watched success all around me. Even my toxic mother was successful. However, no one told me in my formative years how to *keep it*, after making it. I loved achieving goals and, of course, my dreams. Later, I walked past red ropes without anyone knowing my past. I was a mess. I still am, but I decided what life would be.

Perfection and fame is a joke. *You* are the keeper of your *badassism*. Maybe if we had camera phones when I was on tours in the '90s, it would have been nice. Back then I was called dancer no. 2 of the Bizkitettes or chorus girl of the Dolls at the Viper Room. These days, it's what's googleable that counts, right? You, the comment section of actual footage of me on tour with Limp, are still haters. However, as Fred told me, misery loves company and wants to pull us down.

My life is too available, thanks google. More bad than good, because I began messing up after the search engines began.

Yet, I am beyond grateful.

We are all just human. There is space for everyone at whatever table they want. It does take hard work. Dave didn't give me anything. I had to work for it.

CHAPTER 50

Good Morning, Hollywood, Good Night, to the South

We have an Easter morning in Hollywood and an Easter evening in the South. My kids understand and are excited that Mommy is Mommy again (a fighter). They had heard of that fearless girl who became a mom. Moms, we know we are superheroes, but to our babies, we are just a bigger version. They haven't even processed that they grew inside us, and they won't until they have their own children.

So, I laugh. Yet still, I also cry a little inside as my babies grow. I wish we all just "had" it. However, I was either great or horrible at everything my whole life. That includes motherhood. My oldest daughter is a gorgeous, intelligent, driven college student, who at six foot two, is modeling. I chose the industry over my children more than once in the past. Because of this, I have many regrets to this day—related to my favorite yet fickle town. It will connect us with the true emotions, which we all in Hollywood craved. I would again choose work.

I do worry that the lies that surround fame are robbing many people of their courage to step out. Too many are comparing themselves to other *humans. The difference is only determination.* The rest is fake. Many have family ties, clearly, but opportunities are everywhere now.

CHAPTER 51

Yes You Fucking Are…
Just Human

Exhausted, one eye open. Suddenly pausing—a personal glitch. I'm not sure where my fingers would rather be today.

Yet, as I revisit a chapter, looking back then, my eyes "glaze" over. And on and I type my story to you, not knowing who will care or if it matters anywhere. But that God gut we all have, the one that nags at us until we begin, does so even more until we reach the end. Only one person has to see themselves in the "here" pages, and my heart will soar.

I want my children to be kind, even swallowing their pride. However, if we don't advocate for ourselves, who will? I taught my kids to say, "Who raised you to treat others like you are better than anyone?"

Who raised you? What does that bring up?

Some days, having teens, I wonder if they love me anymore. I never used to, until my middle girl Siena started high school. Her smile was so big, and two weeks after ordered, I no longer knew who my baby girl was. She had changed. I *swore* she would love me through anything, personal or public, fatal or superficial wounds (the ones I'd patch up with a nonstick bandage)—until I was no longer allowed near her.

I am sure this book scares them a bit. They know Mommy had a double life at one point. I once dined with drug lords. Then there were my days as a madam for high-class women over what they were, penny whores. I hate that term. We are all human, period, and we should say how we feel—and not with filters that do more than smooth skin or cause some form of perfection. We should be reminding each other that our souls are real.

Many people support me writing this book. One said, "You are the whisper of truth to kids who hopefully will listen and not make the same mistakes. You are spreading more than a story about your past—you're sharing memories of truth." We all have a truth, and most times, it's rooted in fear, pain, and shame. There are many things to hide.

Or we do the opposite—we numb. The grass is rarely greener. However, fulfillment is extremely important. If your middle name is impulsive, as it is mine, try not to make rash decisions. Trust, I still stop and think, *Why, Brooklin? What triggered you with the person, topic, or lack of understanding?* We will never understand anyone fully. It isn't our place. Don't fear mistakes, and imperfections. That is who Jesus loves. It's called the human race. You're already loved. However, you can choose now to change your loss into power. That's purpose in its infancy. You can make a difference while having fun expressing yourself.

Not every part of healing hurts. It's not about who you're supposed to love, what you wear, or if you swear but, rather, what you think and what you say. You can save lives. Start with yours. It's time we think that way! *No more bullshit*! Live authentically.

CHAPTER 52

Once upon Moments in Hollywood

There was a day I landed the role that would have started my acting career. I didn't know how auditions went. I made it clear I had no clue what I was doing. My résumé was shit, blank actually.

I'd had headshots and tear sheets from modeling since I was fifteen. I learned at a young age that being truthful will get you further than lies. Pretending to be something you aren't is not the exact same as choosing not to work it to make it. I wasn't qualified for years. So many lied on paper, and I told the truth and went for it. I lost her until last fall when I finally started writing this book and let *Maxim* happen. I just said fuck it.

We can't wait for it to fall in our laps. It takes a lot of work to get to script heaven.

That day, a sea of faces staring back at me. Then there was me, a fresh-faced, pale brunette with big blue eyes. The year was 2002—before I fucked that up too.

I had the job that day and a strange, demanding, but interesting five weeks on the Universal lot. I was working in true Hollywood, without Daddy's protection. He was proud though.

Filming with Urban, an experiment renowned, successful, and determined group of black artists, still very much in the gam. Though Urban barely lasted a couple of projects. Production company are hard to keep a float. The best are still the ones started when actors were signed and spent five - forever in a contract. It gave them the upper hand, however, made the industry basically a grid like the city is made of. The grid would never change, until the opportunity to flick to Hollywood, as well as social media founding many we know now. My time still was a mix between old fashioned and trying to conform to the new demand. The world was becoming bigger as social media made it so much so. I miss life being smaller, then I think, now I just miss my experience as youth and worry about my children, not having an authenticity in their lives. Travel is no surprise, fraud is on the rise, no conspiracies here, just my few Mommy fears. I will tell you, before social media love and friendship was locked in and the few I had made it through "myspace"

So why Brookie, true girl who was our little homie, yea she is forty and though she knows every damn thing about us. She is kind and would never, so forget the tours, working in the studios I saw crazy shit, the love of my life not responding to me since his birthday and for the first time it was "thx" They stay on the internet and don't have to help you out together a bed or leave their house at all. They find reason to ignore you out of the thief they have been in your life. I was heartbroken after the pandemic, that is when the world was small in our homes, however, bigger on the six sites he was in. My ex. Husband even tried some I have cancer fuck it. I didn't care, so here I stopped, lol.

Lethal is someone I can honestly say was my friend, my Bruh, always there. Never turned me away, until I hurt him, by hurt myself. Eighteen years later I use instagram to send one direct message. I am coming home...

Friends, don't make choices because he or she does and you love them and they you. They say all the right things. High and sober, I promise you, an addict is not faithful to you. How can they be trusted with your heart if they don't reoect themselves.

CHAPTER 53

Don't Burn It Down

Sometimes we want it all to burn down. But the truth still remains, and it always rises from the ashes. We try to walk away from our lives and all that makes it worth it. If we are sufficiently courageous, we don't let what many do burn us—even when they turn on us or reject us.

But many will let us down or worse. We must not let it get to us. Cowards want others' hopes, dreams, and lives to burn down. You, my friend, are more than halfway there. Keep on believing because what you believe is who you are continuing to become. We've all heard this shit before. Then there are those who think, *What I choose to believe or want to disbelieve is up to me*, but then they degrade others along the way.

And certainly don't believe everyone.

The past is a trigger, the present's a place, and the future's a fortune cookie. No one is holy. However, we are all worthy.

CHAPTER 54

The Paps Are Gone...Dude

The paparazzi back then were crazy, and I was a decoy for many. The parties were at a different place every night. So no one, unless they were invited, would know. Bolthouse ran most of the weekly parties. Joseph's was the most important, even on a Monday night. That's Hollywood for you, constantly mingling for your next opportunity.

There were private parties every night—at Spider, Hyde, and Area. Hideaways in Koreatown came much later, like now. There was a code, and tourists would never know where to go. Funny because we were not far from the strip. The Standard, a popular hotel hangout on Sundays on Sunset Strip, is blocks from plenty of tourist attractions. Yet, few knew and stayed at the Saddle Ranch.

Once, AJ and I went there, just to see what fans would do. We regretted trying to get back into his new white Audi. I guess when you're a curious BSB and if they still matter. Make an appearance at a known tourist attraction. Within minutes, the screams and tipped-off paparazzi will fulfill your curiosity. I have pictures from the night, with my hand up. I was trying to get back into the Standard, where I was staying.

Somehow, the parties went on without too many trying to sneak past the huge bodyguards. My personal favorite bodyguards back then were Rob, Moe, and Boom Boom. I'm skipping through time here a little bit. Throughout ten years, I would have my kids off and on. I wasn't the marrying type, always needing to go and do something. When the kids started school, it became harder to be so free. So my ex and I agreed, after pre-K, the kids needed stability. He was retired and willing to provide that, even for me whenever I needed to breathe. Hollywood is exhausting.

Life without my children had me do worse for a while. However, no more than a few months would go by, and I couldn't take it. I would go to be with kids every time. I know many women who won't leave Hollywood. Years pass, and it's clear a career is no longer an option. Yet they hope to meet a rich producer (rare at thirty-nine), while their mom or grandma has their child or children across the country. I don't agree with it personally. However, I do understand the pull of Hollywood.

Losing Lethal and my place in the studio happened first. My addiction slowed down my modeling career, and acting jobs halted. I knew it was time. So I left. I have moved back six times since 1997. I worked for my dad. However, as I've said before, I had so much trauma. I had never spoken of it until 2015.

I kept relapsing over the nightmares and feeling worthless. I just didn't want to feel at all. It would take me until age thirty-three to get my shit together.

Don't let anyone judge you. This is life and there are seasons for everything, especially people, even if they last decades in your life or merely days. Even if you lived your best life together with someone, times change. I always wanted to believe those experiences would bond all of us and keep us easily accessible to each other. When this all started, I was just a teen. I watched a lot of my friends rise to fame—some from the beginning to the end. Some are still on top.

Destiny is a trip.

CHAPTER 55

The Static in My Head

Years later, I still looked the part, while falling apart. Do you feel like that? Your clothes are tailored, you have perfect skin, you're you, but you feel numb.

(That city was hard to wear.) Your looks are your boss. The way you move and how long you can is everything. It became hard to pay attention, much less be on a stage with insecurities that got worse the more I used. However, if I used more I could follow through. It was a vicious cycle. It tricked myself into thinking I was actually living. I was angry at all the static in my head. Still I wasn't ready. I was in love and intrigued by my town, I will say.

Learn to read a room like a computer. Don't expect anything from hardly anyone.

CHAPTER 56

Fame Is an Illusion

Sure, I've run from paparazzi with Fred, Leo, Linds, just HUMANS. We'd get to my place, they'd raid my fridge, blow up my bathroom, try on everything in my closet (I worked in the wardrobe on music video sets, so I had a badass collection of vintage clothes). We'd smoke and talk about the end of the world (just people). I know when you accomplish what only 1 percent of the population does, it is something to look up to.

I was asked recently during a live podcast promoting this almost finished book, "What moment would you say was the moment you realized my first dream was accomplished?" Then did something was the next question? I haven't done it yet.

Though, My answer of accomplishment? "When on stage in front of thousands, as a dancer with Limp. I'll never forget that feeling, like it was yesterday.

Again not fame…today you don't have to leave your house. Back then you did.

Back then, we had "Pink Dot" only, a simple delivery service with a small menu of pre-made meals and groceries. No Instacart, like today. And stillq no google.

I understand the wonderment of the whole vision or idea of "celebrity." However, remember that celebrities are just people. The paps have become even more out of control. It is their job to give you a view of perfection (or not). It gets old. Not everyone is asking for it. Actors love their craft. Musicians love their music. That's no secret.

Just human and all going through something. When they raided my fridge, it made me go through something. I didn't like leaving my penthouse, not for fame, from laziness. I was on the twelfth floor with a perfect view of the Hollywood sign. My penthouse was quite popular. But it was on the twelfth floor, and parking in LA is a bitch. So I ordered Pink Dot too. Now I'm an Instacart junkie, versus the other kind.

Chapter 57

Stevie and Dad Jokes

Dad and I had just left SIR studios, after he nixed a Linkin wannabe. We were actually about to induct Linkin on the RockWalk anyway. Dad had this thing when he was over a viewing. He would look at his watch and then me and say, "Damn it I can't see, and we have a meeting with Stevie."

I would gasp.

They'd meet at dad's office or home studio. Stevie was very private. It was the day before Christmas Eve, and he wanted to have a quiet time and feel and hear the new pro-tools. Here comes my dad with dad jokes. He says, "Stevie, have a look around."

I cradled my head and put one hand on Stevie.

Quicker than my eyes were rolled, Stevie said, "Tell your dad to shut the fuck up." And they laughed.

About two hours and four coffees later, that latter which I ran and bought almost hourly (Daddy made me work), Stevie found his revenge. He drove my dad's coveted Mercedes while reminding him he was blind the whole time.

I just laughed at two men who would never grow up. This was another surreal moment in my life. I couldn't believe this was my life. My dad's fame had risen a lot in the past decade, but he hadn't changed a bit. He had true friendships and an actual rolodex he kept up with.

It was making their dreams come true. That, to me, is life fulfilled, and that, my friends, is fucking life!

CHAPTER 58

Ugh, a Madam: Really? (Damn it)

I almost forgot this part of my messy life. I am ashamed of it now. At the time, I thought I was helping women. Some were runaways, and I made sure my clients were wealthy. I did this for almost four years in an apartment off Wilshire. I had a partner who carried on when I was in my other home in Georgia—if it got hot especially.

However, finally in 2014, I was arrested for trafficking women, which really threw me off. I never ever thought I was doing something so vile. It turns out the DA was on my rolodex, so they let me go on a lesser charge, which was later expunged. But I was in jail for more than thirty days. Let's just say that scared me. And I was less of a madam after that and, as a friend worded it the other day, more of a matchmaker.

Damn it, I was a madam. I think of all the things I have done because trauma makes nothing seem as if it is "too bad" or will have consequences. Why would it? When I was ten, I was abused, and nothing happened.

It wasn't until my daughter was diagnosed with cancer that I opened my eyes. My daughter was now facing her first trauma. After I got past the shock and went into beast mode, never leaving that hospital for weeks, then I became angry. My mother wasn't as concerned for my pain. How is that possible? Then I reminded myself

Thigh Highs and No Lies

the blame game wasn't going to do anything but keep me angry. We move forward. Many things from my past and people I hung with or thought cared about me now make me cringe. But we move forward. When the memories creep up, I literally shake them off. I move forward and remember I don't have to be that person ever again.

I am not immune to bad decisions. I have to keep my guard up. We all slip. For me, it can be depression that gives me trouble when it comes to having the normal life I've been given. I tell myself the past is over. I knew not was I was doing. If I could go back in time, there is much I would do differently. But I can't. So I do my best and shake it off, while moving forward.

Madam? They were runaways.

What work is done? What do most people in Hollywood eat? (Not much.) I love gluten-free grilled cheese though.

After I turned twenty-seven, modeling slowed down. During that time, I went to school and became an esthetician. My dad always said have a normal plan B. So, skincare after modeling, acting, and dancing. It made sense.

I was working on my psychology degree and spoke at churches about my trauma. Child Advocacy called me to come and assist children to talk in a safe place. Trust, someone was scaring them or not believing them. I'd been there. Both things were going to scare a child. With me, I'd ask the kids to draw pictures and talk about how we relate. No one is alone. That is what this book is really about—whether I'm talking about what happened to me, going to jail, or almost being sentenced to two years for being a madam. (the charge was trafficking women.) That broke my heart, as I thought I was helping keep girls off the street. I didn't talk. Then like the heavens opening or our corrupt system doing what it does—God, America is fucked—the DA ended up being in my "rolodex." When I say it that way, it makes me feel horrible. I believed I was helping runaways who would do it anyway.

I ran one of my businesses off of Wilshire with a friend who shall remain nameless. Her dad was also a music producer, who loved the Playboy mansion. I was uncomfortable, scared. His daughter was no joke, but we partnered and, for three years, had a business. She kept it going after my arrest and retirement. (I say retirement.) My high-level Hollywood lawyer took care of me. I met her through her dad, who founded PRC, a rehabilitation center I attended twice.

How did I get arrested? One of my girls went rogue and went to a hotel with doors on the outside. I taught my girls never do that. Have a card to get in the damn elevator. She said she was scared, and it was my job to protect them. Thought it felt off, I came to help her. I went to Koreatown—which was some bullshit in itself. I *knew* deep down I was being set up. I told John, my driver and bodyguard, "If I scream, peel off. I won't speak." My dad told me to never snitch when I was young. Was he proud I got involved in that world now? No. But there is gangsta in our blood and the underworld too.

We all have pasts. Judge if you must, but know I won't tolerate it.

Did I need the money? No. Having a seat at the men's table was what I was really craving. I really thought I was helping girls who would have been on the street otherwise. I found some on backlist, but it all started with one girl crying in the bathroom of a party. I will never do it again. However, one of my girls married a producer and is living a very large life in Bel Air. They have two kids. She is spoiled and is happily grateful. All she wanted was to be rich if modeling and acting didn't work, and she is.

So it wasn't for greed or all for nothing.

I truly believed these girls were safe.

Oh, and no I never talked. I didn't have to. Like I said, the DA was in my rolodex. They let me go, afraid I could or would ruin his life. Hollywood, you rub my back, and I'll rub yours. Or get me the fuck out of being locked up and I'll stay quiet. That was the business. Hush. Still is.

Chapter 59

Dr. Phil's Experience

Apparently, it was a shit show. However, during commercial breaks, Dr. Phil was very kind. And he sent me where I needed to go—a rehab for sexual trauma only—and got me off Subutex. My episode aired and was one of the longest running on Oprah's channel, OWN. Later, she gave me a paid partnership on Instagram for inspiring others. That was the beginning of more than my wheels turning for this book. It still would take five more years to start. Dr. Phil's people have checked in here and there. His divorce shocked us all and him the most. His sons are a great support.

I am grateful to him, though his TV persona is different from who he is during commercial breaks. He was always concerned and began to realize something had happened to me—and also that something was off with my mother. So he sent me to Willow House, which saved me. It was there that I was finally seen and understood. At Willow House in the hills of Arizona, there were no comparisons, only kindness and understanding, with the most beautiful sunrises and sunsets I'd ever seen.

As a tiny side note of gossip, Harvey Wienerstein came for three hours, and his pride took over and there his limo went. Spacey stayed the whole time. You see, pride is truly the fall of all falls. I know personally and will never out anyone by name. I am, however, disgusted with pride. I had a podcast set up with some random podcast Label Free, and my daughter took a bad turn with her blindness and cancer. And the cruelty and lack of understanding that I was met with on canceling over a week in advance reminded me. Always stay humble. The nice guy doesn't finish last; he lasts longer.

CHAPTER 60

Unlearning What I Was Taught: My Dad's Humility

Hollywood is full of whispers and a lack of humility. Dad always felt his main job was to keep me grounded. It wasn't always so, and quite a lot would assume otherwise. They would be wrong. Fame is an illusion, as much as shame is. Hollywood is full of both. One, we are all the same. And two, we've all had shame and pain.

What would you want, fame or money (if one didn't mean the other anymore)?

I must tell you, before Nikki; Paris; and, of course, the Kardashians, it wasn't the same. No hard feelings or shame in your game. However, I miss those days.

A close friend once asked, "So, you have a famous dad?

There are many questions that will be answered here. I also get asked where I have been the last twenty-five years since I left Europe. It's not quite that simple. I never had a dad, really. I had a sister who took most of the responsibilities and chose to take care of me. Even my older brother was there before he finally had to leave. I was fifteen when I moved in with my sister in Los Angeles.

I spent my time racking up phone bills to psychics and calls to my best friend Jessamyn in Maryland. I was bored. That was before I realized my older sister would let me do my own thing. She was living it up.

That would be the heart of Hollywood. She was hanging out with Pauly for a while. He lived in the known pink house above the Comedy Store. The parties were wild in the late '90s. (I loved it.)

The best part is the grace life will give you eventually. If it wasn't for my sister, I never would have met my dad or partied in the pink house at fifteen and skated down to Sunset Boulevard, literally smacking entirely into Seth (Shifty). We both fell, as you can imagine. He was with Pep, Spoon, and Bernard. B helped me up while laughing hysterically. That moment became two days of tattoos and studio time. I met "him". To this day, he says, "You are literally everywhere." Well, I was until 2018.

As you know, times have changed rapidly since the pandemic. I had also left Hollywood nine months before the pandemic, because my then eight-year-old told me something was wrong. I had two dreams of her reaching for me, so I left my dream job at Netflix in Hollywood.

CHAPTER 61

Dad's Sunset Boulevard Office: A Lifeline

At Dad's office, almost every day someone you may call famous walked in. Slash was the first, I soon began calling him Hudson, because I like full names and to know people. He will always be Slash, but he is Hudson to me. He was not only kind, he and dad had a special friendship.

Let's get to the part when I figured out who Dave Weiderman really was, besides his humility and driving the same Mercedes for fifteen years. He's from South Side, Chicago, and stayed pretty conscious of spending money.

I tell him today he saved my life, and he did. Life lessons were always summoned up with being honest and humble throughout life. To be honest, his biggest problem with my mother is she didn't teach me either of those things. I had many time-outs in his office. (Not bad for a time-out, by the way.) Don't tell Dave that. Dad founded more than the RockWalk and Melissa Ethridge. He founded trust in a town with everyone who knew him. He had an ear for not just music but also determination. We bonded over that fascination. My time-outs consisted of going through demos and weeding out what I believed to be good or bad new music. Linkin Park came across his desk and into my ear, as did Limp and Staind. Many I had to convince my dad were the new rock. He agreed.

Years and tours later, Dad inducted Linkin Park on the RockWalk, but not before he made connections and more opportunities for them. He connected tons of collaborations between different music genres over the years. I know this chapter jumps around. However, that's life in that town.

Almost everyone came to my dad for advice for lifelong choices and investments in and outside of music. He called me in the early 2000s and randomly told me, "Fifty Cent may be the smartest in this town. You watch."

Like any daughter I was like, "K, Dad."

He was always right. I still stand corrected by him daily.

Robert Knight, the former photographer for Lynyrd Skynyrd in the late '60s and '70s, was a close friend of Dad's and gave him the coolest fifty-fifth birthday gift—original photography from Woodstock, including a blast from that past. The shot was of my dad with Jimi Hendrix and the Roots. Great. How was I gonna top that? Well he wore the shoes I bought him every day. (He loves Italian leather custom-made shoes to this day.)

I started figuring out, Dad didn't run just any guitar store. It was *the* guitar store. My dad was the best at managing, producing, and public relations. You can imagine how much I began to learn and how quickly. Then one day, not long after one of my first days at Dad's office "he" walked in. We were cool. I was the manager's daughter. I was young. But sparks flew and dad knew.

"He" snuck me smokes, and we just hung out. He has always been available until weeks ago. But this is my life.

By this point, I figured out my dad was more than the head of the most popular store for rock stars. It even went beyond him being the founder of the RockWalk when I was four in 1985. The year my mom took me far away, to Germany, where I would remain until I was fifteen. The RockWalk his creation on Sunset Boulevard. It's pretty dope and a tourist attraction daily. He was a humble Grammy-nominated producer. I did spend my teenage and young adult years working in famous studios with him. They included Capitol, Lethal Dose, SUR, and Apex, along with some hole-in-the-wall studios most walk past, never knowing the magic being made. Dad also had a studio in his home. I was surrounded by music and musicians from the age of fifteen through now, off and on. This was a life That wasn't comparable to the one I'd gladly left in Europe.

Chapter 62

Coming Forward

My coming forward will almost certainly break up relationships in my life—especially with those who know the truth and the ones who will think they do because I never told them. And to that handful, I simply say, fuck you. Tell your own story or give a fuck. But the truth takes more courage and guts than the lies and bullshit I've lived with. I know life isn't fair, which is why there is now whining. I just hope some are set free. The world can be just, if you have the will and strength to be up for any fight—even against those who are supposed to love you.

Love is fickle. I learned that the hard way. I have kept quiet long enough. I was approached to write a book about my life in the mid 2000s. No one, much less me, knew what this would be. I was still afraid then, not anymore. This is the first book. We chose nonfiction first. Get to know me. There are others. All include experiences I have had. Some are based in Hollywood and cover the fun stuff. Others are on drug use and the darkness I endured, even months in prison.

It was time for this story. The last person I was protecting was my grandmother, and she passed two and a half years ago. The first time the story is about "my life," not only being an NBA wife or life in recovery. A close friend said, "Stop mumbling to yourself about the past of Brooklin. Quit whispering. It's time to tell it, the truth. Kids, women, men, everyone needs to hear someone speak out."

Me? I thought. "Why?"

She replied, "Because you have the balls to, so just do it." She went on, "Maybe, they won't make the same mistakes or take the same paths, so many paths you took, Brooke."

Don't I know it.

CHAPTER 63

How Does Prison Become Paradise?

Like Henry Tudor with his wives, many won't care when I am gone. That's OK. This book isn't about that. Many of these memories formed in vivid stories. Some are exactly in order, and some will be scattered. Not many of these stories are exactly a legacy. I am no Krishna or Mother Teresa. I am many things and have been many more. I don't know how this book will be compared to others. We all have our own words and way of expressing ourselves. This first line sounds strange. But if you have been reformed, you will understand. If you haven't, think of the things that imprison you and how those very things can set you free. Walk with me down another fucking memory lane another lifetime ago. This was 2013 to 2015. It began in 2012 and ended with me being released from prison in 2015. I was only locked up for seventy-two days. But the saga lasted too long, and that was how it ended—which drugs and bad choices will do. I should be dead by many accounts. I used to wonder why I survived.

I don't anymore. We are here to do something, and I will keep doing something no matter if I fail or not. I won't stop. We can't. We have to keep going, we have no choice. At least, that is how we should all be thinking. I know it's hard. I have laid in bed for months at a time—even when I was out of jail, not still imprisoned.

How did prison resemble Paradise?

Thigh Highs and No Lies

What is the bondage of prison, the limits, the actual bonds you make? And then what if you get another chance at your freedom?

I have been locked up and freed before.

The strong women in prison I met were freer than me there than on the outside. Yet, there are no limits. Surprisingly, in prison, there was camaraderie; acceptance; and, yes, mutual understanding. We fucked up.

My charges would suddenly be dropped, almost three months into my sentence. I will never forget when they said, Brooklin, pack it up. You're going home"

I was having coffee with some of the other women on my cell block before lights out. I know, coffee before lights out, always the rebel.

I had been booked for trafficking women seventy-two days earlier. Technically, I was a madam. There is a difference when you aren't exploiting girls. I'm telling this story because Google is a bitch, and people will find shit. So, let me tell you how it all went down. There is no defending trafficking. But that isn't close to what I was a part of. If you saw my rolodex, you probably wouldn't be shocked that the DA set me free. Why? Because I had shit on him obviously. He, a married Southern gentleman who was on his month vacation, realized this as soon as he found out I was Brooklin, his lady of the night booker. And because I wouldn't talk to the interrogator about shit.

Look, my dad always said, "Do the time if you have any part in the crime." I wasn't trafficking women, but I needed my ass sat the fuck down for other things.

I was there because I was answering a bugged call of the twenty-year-old girl I saved two years earlier. She was eighteen when I met her at my friend Scout's. He was a drug dealer and close friend. He wasn't your typical dealer. He was kind, funny, and a protective person for the three years we did business. This girl came in one day while I was making him and his friends spaghetti in his nice midtown apartment. She was bruised and battered and spoke with a heavy Southern drawl. She wasn't from around here was all I knew. She was like a lost puppy at the door and knew my nickname, "Madame B". That was code—she's cool. So I let her in, to the guys' glares and chagrin. She was young, only a few years older than my oldest child. I took my time measuring the heroin she asked for. She only had twenty-five dollars. The guys knew I was taking too long. It was my God gut being tugged.

I might not have been locked up for the right crime, but I was locked up at the right time. As I measured out dope for a child, I felt sick. I didn't like participating in the dealing until I realized it gave me power and a seat at the table. Drug money runs through almost everything, friends. I learned more about life being a dealer than I did going to college for psychology.

I began talking to her, offering her food and clothes. She was a beautiful girl. She told me hastily she'd run away from home, and someone told her there was a nice woman who dealt dope. "The men made me pay with sex, beat me, gang-raped me, and then shot me up. They didn't leave me anything except the clothes on my back."

I asked her how she had the twenty-five she was giving me for this dope.

And she said, "Backlist."

I had no clue what she meant. She leaned in to whisper this. That mixed with her Southern drawl and my four black friends sitting at the table playing cards within earshot made me think, it was possibly racist at first. My face flushed and I looked her in the face and said, "How old are you? Where did you come from, because we don't talk like that around here?"

Scout came over and asked what was up, and I said, "All good," while I watched this girl cower when a harmless black man approached.

Scout was handsome, my height, and lighter skinned than the other three. He was funny and carried wads of cash just to see if someone tried anything. It made me laugh. He accused me once as a test, after leaving my house, as he usually would deliver. However, when he realized I was smart and trustworthy, he wanted me around to help make decisions.

This decision I was about to make would change the dynamic of everything I had ever done and every line I had crossed. But as she told me her story, my heart broke. I asked about her mother.

Her whimpered reply, "She doesn't care," broke my heart.

It also had my mind swirling with thoughts—not just the obvious. I'm going to have to fix that improper grammar. Then the mother in me sprung to action. With a quick evaluation of questions, I gathered that she had no phone and nowhere to go, except this blacklist online, where men would prowl her ad. And once I saw her pitiful self and horribly written bio, it was clear why she was getting the type of clientele she was attracting.

My business mind kicked in. I knew I could fix this, but first I would need to talk to her mother. We called from my phone, this tiny eighteen-year-old, who looked like the girl next door. Her mother picked up without a care in the world—this after her daughter had been missing for three weeks. "She graduated high school?" her mother asked.

I said, "*And* she is penniless, dope sick, and beat up. Should I send her home?"

Her mother went on as if she hadn't heard me. "I have a new boyfriend, and he wants just me. Listen," she said, "clearly I was a teen mom. I am done."

I told her, "Your daughter was at one of my apartments beaten up, on drugs, and she's been on a sex website for the past two weeks at least." I was hoping she'd missed that detail two minutes earlier. I went on, explaining what I knew, "That means the $250 you gave her got her to Atlanta from Charleston because she was told rich men were here. She has no guidance or understanding and won't make it in this town. I will send her home, ma'am."

She said, "No she ain't." (Well, there it was—the lack of articulation and, worse, love.) Even a diploma had her speaking like her uneducated selfish mother. She was all alone.

I told her mother, "I'm a mother, and you should be ashamed. I have daughters, and what has happened to her would get me put away once I found the disgusting humans that did this to another human."

Her mother said one last thing before I hung up, heated as hell. She said, "Welp, it's that there website she got on, and it was her decision too."

Oh I wished she was the one black and blue in front of me. But it wasn't. It was a shattered little girl. She was a version of me, who had been hurt and abused too. But my family had money and fame, which makes coverups easy and offers lots of opportunity to bury the pain.

She had nothing. I was thirty-one and was also using heroin as maintenance. My body was addicted, but I was done. It would take me two more years to finally stop. That jail stop was right on time, and it was because of this girl and the decision I was about to make. I didn't just keep my business in Atlanta either. I took it back to LA to an apartment on Wilshire, with a partner whose father was also a producer. Fleiss had passed her rolodex down to the customer's kid. Oh, this web goes deep my friends. But this book will exceed the word count, and frankly, my time is up to tell you the most poignant parts of my life.

I am staying pretty much on the surface; with loads of memories, you will be able to generate your own opinions, visuals, and thoughts.

These are the ones I was led to share. I pondered this one. It's tricky. Do I tell you all the details after I got her cleaned up and convinced one of the biggest kingpins in town to rent me two apartments over the course of the next two years (after I got off the phone with another devil woman for a mom)? Do I wake up the dead past to live to see the light of day? These were some of my darkest days. These dark days were my choice. So it is only fair to tell you my fair share of horrible misconduct.

I had this shaky girl who I knew was also addicted, and to help her I would have to invest in what she muttered. "I can do it best."

Before I walked back from the table, my guys were eavesdropping while counting cash and shaking their heads, knowing I was about to save a ho again. I hate that term, but that is what they said. They weren't unkind. They just didn't fuck with girls who ended up like that. I promised I would fix her up and talk to Tiger, who ran things at a different location every day. Few knew where he was, but I did.

If you are wondering how I managed to get in deep everywhere I went and find a way to be at the big boys' table in various career endeavors, I am told it's my ability to articulate and learn quickly; but most of all, it's about loyalty and trust. It's about never judging anyone, except devilish, uncaring moms. First step, did she want my help and was this what she wanted?

The answers to both were yes. She needed to make money and fast. Ugh, OK. So, after a few minutes of research, I changed her profile to a better site. Then I called Tiger with my plight.

He said, Brooklin, I gotchu. Just don't fuck it up, and we split 75 percent. That's it. We will reconvene when you make more than $1,000 in two days on her."

We doubled that by adding "packages." I treated it like a high-class spa from day one. I got her cleaned up and in new lingerie and a sexy girls' school uniform. I knew she would be that girl for the men. And she got days-of-the-week panties because that was requested.

CHAPTER 64

I Channel It Differently Now

My heart's desire to help those in trauma or over trauma hasn't changed. I just channel it differently from experience, not being stupid or entirely reckless like I was back then. If Slim, as we called her, hadn't gone rogue on "Backlist" after two years of my pampering, things would have been different. By then, there was a team of people assembled as the operation grew to no more than four of five girls at a time, who had a driver and bodyguards and aa call curfew. I supplied them with phones that were to be for personal use only and burners for clients. They were discreet meets, escorted by my driver to their dates. The driver would wait not far from the door with their own card. This was a mandatory rule and in my contract, signed by all clients—including the DA a few counties over, who got me out as soon as he knew I was actually "Madame B"

"What can I do for you?"

I didn't want to threaten, but I made it clear, if he wasn't reached, he was the only one I would ever speak of. We had a deal to protect me if this happened. When it did, I was in the damn South. an hour away from his jurisdiction. It took him a month just to convince the opposing DA he wanted my case because my operation was in the city, and he had been watching too. Could've fooled that country town, we saw my girl only three times frequent this one piece-of-shit hotel for a pastor who promised her the world and paid well. He paid so well, he gave her up not to lose his church. We took care of that.

Word travels fast when you fuck me over. He could've said it was an affair. They wouldn't have known.

However, it was the driver "John", who she was sucking off for more drugs, who went behind my back too. And the cue was to drive off if I screamed a certain word. "*Fuuuucckkkkk*" (whatever it worked, and they lost him). It was a straight-up sting. The whole time, he drove me there because she said, "I'm scared," he was aware it was a sting.

The only reason he was let go without a scratch for betraying me was that he was right. I wouldn't sing like our little hurt bird. When I got out of prison, I never went back to any of those places or saw those faces. I let Nikki take over "Wilshire". Last I heard, it was still up and running from the same high-rise, with my rolodex, no doubt. One of my girls was divorced with two kids from the "Persian" producer she trapped. Though she's living in a mansion, their traditions have kept her slightly imprisoned as far as I know.

There are never fairy tales, especially when they begin with deceit. I don't believe I ruined anyone's life. Half of them friended me on social media and congratulated me on things I do or when my daughter, two then, now twelve, survived cancer. The streets don't call me anymore. They never really did.

What called me was the path I was meant to follow. I deviated and was disciplined. Then I was set free like nothing happened. That lesser charge is a reminder of what I was really a part of, not who I was. I wasn't even fully aware what it felt like to be called a prostitute until that lesser charge. Now, it's off my record.

Not hiding this time of my life is the least I can do to tell this story from an insider's point of view—to show where trauma can take you.

I am not a victim anymore, but I still was then. It was a time in my life that still disgusts me—not the girls or what I thought it all stood for. I feel for the wives and children of these "gentlemen," all with badges or awards of some sort. Every one of my clients were successful at what they did. Yep, some are to this day. One owns the nicest hotels in Atlanta, the ones I told my girls to use exclusively. The doors are inside. The elevator requires a key. And usually those hotels have tinted windows and deal with the people who arrested me and set me free. This whole world is full of wild scenarios. Somehow, I have seen almost all of them. As a child, I was raped and neglected. Even seeing war and the "Wall" coming down always stuck with me. I would be sitting in my high-rise with plenty of money; friends; what I thought was love; jobs; and, my downfall, dope. Yet, I would listen to "Oasis" "Wonderwall" and remember that wall and the visions of people running in fear they would still be shot, their families once a few blocks away. They were separated overnight by a quiet communist regime for twenty-five years—a regime who spun a barbed wire fence up in complete silence and darkness. Let that sink in.

Imagine all the things that still go on in the darkness—whether it is night or not. I know if I stepped foot back in one of those penthouses I essentially ran as a little empire, I would get physically ill. My whole continence would change. I would immediately feel fear, knowing I was living wrong. Back then, I truly believed in that reality. I wasn't hurting anybody. I saw my children almost daily. The girls had everything they needed. The deal sounds like shit on their end, though. They got tips, jewelry, a few cars eventually, and their bills paid—down to their hair, nails, and spray tans. I even had a few Botox parties for them. I thought I was Mama Bear, and I was to them.

But I had my own children. And God forbid if they were ever in that situation—even treated well. I know these women were lonely as hell, because I also kept them maintained with what they needed. They all came to me addicted. Again, so was I. So after all that, I went to the county and then transferred to the city prison, so I could be let out in Mr. DA's jurisdiction within two days. I never saw a judge or him again.

My probation was paid, and I got a short letter that read, "It is done. Please walk away. I paid everything off so you can have a clean slate. You are a good woman who I respect. Forgive me for taking so long, Brooklin No more lies. Go live more lives." He then wrote, "This was just a disguise. I saw your real life, and this whole time you were like me, living very comfortably and with a famous background. But like me, something pulled you down. You're free,

Thigh Highs and No Lies

don't fuck up or mention me by name. But I will never forget you, "Madame B".

I still had that note. I don't know why. I shredded it because it was a reminder too close to home. I am telling you the surface of the story though. There was way more involved and people this world relies on, and yet, they can't help themselves. It was almost a case study on my abuser when it was done. I realized they aren't well. They call and want this age, or for their date to dress young, not this or that. By far, young was the most important.

Now, the girls all have kids, and two are married and seem OK. Two are divorced, and only one got what she wanted—wealth and freedom. She was a gorgeous mixed model in LA. If anyone was going to be a trophy, it was her, and she gave up all her aspirations for four years of faking it and two gorgeous kids—all to live in Beverly Hills doing her thing. She thanked me a few times, but we don't talk anymore.

It feels inappropriate to me to have anything to do with my past self, "Madame B." She wasn't real, but this entire book is as real as I can be. I shared lives with cellmates, AA participants, and celebrities. Even my children prefer to remain partly anonymous, until we get through this book and see what people think. They are young adults and a toddler. They deserve to have that right. Mommy embarrasses them by wearing leather and no bra still. Secretly, they love having a young, tattooed mom, but other moms are either afraid of me or think I am too free. Well, this might make them think I was an angel before. I have harmless doves, angel wings, and my children's name wrapped in cherry blossoms across my body, and initials devour my ankles. I find ink to be art, and those who have them, too, wear their hearts on the outside. Pay more attention to those inked-up folks. See what they wrote down for an artist to permanently place across them for the world to see.

"Belle âme" (beautiful soul) was my most recent.

I wouldn't have gotten that a decade ago. I felt dirty and worthless. I poured myself in whatever character the world had me play. I know I took a lot on myself. But to this day, I would never turn a beaten, cold, hungry, addicted girl away. I would just handle it differently. I had chosen to become a psychologist quietly to learn more about the human mind after what happened to me. My mother was the main reason I hid it. Also, my oldest daughter was working through a lot of anger with me. She didn't see me use or have wild parties, but she was old enough when I got locked up to be ashamed. My arrest made the evening and morning news because of who I was related to. Again, that is enough of then.

Now, I am far away from that life. I am nowhere near where I want to be, but I am nowhere near where I was. I don't know where life is taking me with this book. I do know I have been sitting down nearly every day and writing down memories near and far. I've recorded memories that have made me stop and cry for days, losing friends who were unphased by me being an addict or a madam. Even after I got out of prison and through losing everything a few times, I still had a solid crew. That is, I did until I started this book.

My mind definitely went through some seriously overwhelming phases, and I was deeply nervous at the beginning. I sent specks of chapters to people who I thought were lifelong friends. I lost two almost immediately, due to me being too intense. I always was; the drugs mute you. We are messy creatures just trying to make it. If you make it to the place you don't have to be the center of attention, you're doing all right.

Now, in saying that, this book is not intended to glamorize or advocate making any of these choices. They were dangerous, and I had stalkers and my life threatened a few times. I was just numb and would tell them where to put the gun; the four times I was held at gunpoint, they called me crazy and ran. Was I scared? Once, I was early pregnancy and was terrified, but I still wouldn't give in. And you, motherfucker, will not be raping me and my baby, so shoot me then. He ran too.

That's my personality. And to this day I will take a bullet for anyone. I'd rather it be me. Pain and trauma are so hard to recover from. One thing God gave me was resilience and a sense of knowing I am not done. When I am, he will tell me, and I will go peacefully, praying for my babies, their faces flashing before my eyes. But what I won't have is regret, because I fucking tried. I wasn't given the best start, but I was given a big heart; and it gets overwhelming for some who I have loved. I have cared for more than I can count. But love, the kind you can't do without? Including my children, there are nine human lives I love to this day and always will. That doesn't mean they even still love me or acknowledge me anymore.

But the truth of life is a revolving door. Some keep passing through for more of you, time, advice, laughs, habit, obsession. Others still stand on the other side watching but are too afraid to walk through the front door. They sneak in quietly, and we let them because we are afraid of something too. Or Is it that we see ourselves in them?

CHAPTER 65

The One Who's Like a Mirror

The ones who are like a mirror are your other half. You shape each other by getting rid of the other's trash. It doesn't have to be exhausting, but it is. Or it can be. It's a choice. So many stay on the outside and never change or feel the love the universe intended for them, aimlessly wandering, with random people swearing they hate you. Yet, they're wondering why they're doing what they're doing while watching you, whether every time they close their eyes or when it's quiet, you pop up in their mind.

It happens to me, and I want it to stop too. But it doesn't because it isn't supposed to. For whatever reason, I am supposed to want to love them anyway. I realized a long time ago, no daydreams ever come out of looking at life that way. However, direct your energy on what it stands for. If you see them happy, that's the universe telling you to hope for those things for them—to stop praying for it to be you they see. Pray for happiness in their life. And whoever is there, thank the universe that they're OK and peaceful.

That's what we wanted with them, right? It wouldn't be fair to not wish for their happiness regardless, or it wasn't love. Don't worry about them. Say your hopes and affirmations. And say their name for all those things, and you will most likely receive what you hoped for in some form.

CHAPTER

66

If God Doesn't Recognize Him for You

Like my dad says, you have to give to receive. If I am not recognized by someone who God chose for me to believe in and care for, most likely, we aren't equally tied to the same system. I am ruled by the love of God through me. Without that, I am nothing. Even with my bad decisions and still imperfections, I acknowledge that I can't do anything fully without him guiding me. Spirituality is not a church, and there is only one rule. Know how to humble yourself and ask for forgiveness of anyone, because you will need it. This world and those in it are here to test you and push your buttons.

Will you stay or will you go when your eyes can see into me, and yet that friction that makes us both better people and the forgiveness extended grows us? And if you stayed a while or came by any given day and peeked into my life more regularly and openly, let me speak to all of you.

Let's imagine what would happen if more people would unfuck themselves and see the other person as a human, asking themselves why they are drawn to the other and taking away the judgment that makes everyone nervous and uneasy. Does someone remind you of your messy integrity and your own insecurities? Then look again at that person who bugged you for simply caring or just trying to make a point. Ignore the noise and what others say. Half of it is bullshit and most likely because they didn't get laid. The other is the envy of this world. Unconditional love. A fairytale, I know no doesn't exist.

My strong love for God seems curious to some. It is the only unconditional love of all. I had to have it explain this to me over and over again, as well, because I felt unworthy. stupid, unattractive, and dumb for caring so much for someone I can't always call. You can always call on the Universe/God. Human love, some days, he answers on the first ring or texts back in seconds. Other times, days, hours, or weeks go by before he acknowledges me again. I don't know why or frankly care. Maybe he was in a relationship for a while. And he has said when we spend six hours a day texting, it's like a relationship, and I won't move back; so he's frustrated. So we fight, and I don't handle them well apart.

A gun to my head, I can see it all happening. Communication from far away gets misconstrued, and people get confused. If you are like me, you wanted answers for too long. And suddenly you wake up and say, "Fuck, why did I do that? If it were now, I would stay cool and chill out."

Everything happens for a reason. Learning to forgive is the greatest lesson in life, along with learning not to judge and to really pay attention to who was there through the most. He wrote a song and it said "final backout." I knew that meant me. We had been trying to figure out where we both were in life and why, if we were so far apart, did it even matter.

Everything matters in your life. Some things matter more than others, and some ones more than others. Just remember what I say in this book a number of times. Life is constantly moving—not just the globe we are on but also the axis in which it turns takes our energy and thoughts to the person you are thinking of. Sometimes, you will reach out to them or they may reach out or post something oddly eerie and it hits you, that exact moment I was speaking life into your space.

I think of all these horrible things I've done—not knowing it has led me to be so much more compassionate, especially after being a madam. I think of how many men married to beautiful caring woman who you would never think they would jeopardize that for a lunch-hour fuck with a stranger.

I have never been cheated on—unless the relationship was ending anyway, and I was no saint either. I have gone between two men for twenty-three years, plus sprinkle in one for three and a half years; and they all knew. I was faithful to two fully. It's the one who I have trouble with too.

So, I see the dilemma of eternal bachelorhood, the allure of not having to answer to anyone. But like Mr. DA said, I have it all too. And something pulled me into needing more. And I am done. He realized a few texts and being kind will get you exactly what you want every time. You drive a wedge because you can't make up your mind. Or maybe it's because that person seems unreachable in such an annoying way you bicker just to have something to say.

No matter what I did in my past and the women I took the charge for and, on paper, was a prostitute. So what? Who cares? I am still me, and I've lived a lot of lives. I wish a lot of things were different. But they are the way they are. People choose to believe what they want about me. It's unfortunate anyone would choose to be hateful, to accuse you of things that are not true. They will call you names because they didn't get what you got, as I have been bullied for numerous things. They don't know you unless they want to.

My decisions even last month are not ones I would make today. I am constantly learning and growing from choices I consciously make. I know I can still be a mess who has two sides, and one is being tamed daily. She is wild, fearless, too honest, and has bad timing. Then there is me—the one so few take the time to know, past my anxiety or excitement depending. They don't realize, when you judge me, I shut down and become a blubbering idiot. I just don't speak that language. I have been known to speak too much and cut people off. If one of you is reading this, know it's because I don't see you enough and wanted to get it all out. Or my emotions took me by surprise, and I got lost in the eyes of the past and assumed I still mattered just the same. And people change. I don't know many loyal people there are. I am loyal to a fault. I forgive and forget because, fuck, have you read these pages? Who the fuck am I?

I do have a huge fault shared by many—defensiveness. I had to constantly defend myself growing up from being unloved by the one person who is supposed to love you regardless. My kids are my true loves. I am not always present, I admit. As an artist, I climb into my spot and will zone out for hours or until my bladder is about to pop. I get dehydrated from not being able to stop what I'm doing. Is there a means to an end of this autobiography of an almost forty-one-year-old now? I fucking hope so. Nine and a half months—anyone who is a mother knows it's time to be induced. Every day, I think I'm done. God says, nope, someone may need this.

I say, "God no. It's lame and pointless."

But did I learn. Did I grow? Were there consequences you all may benefit from knowing? For the record, the DA got me off, but I still sat there with a sentence of two years, having no idea if anyone was going to help me. I had gone and done it that time. Regardless, I am not a failure, and I moved forward. And we all have the opportunity to do that. I know they say put foot in front of the other. But I say start with your thoughts. Put your mind to it. Then you will get it done. Or you will end up like me, in the laundry room or pantry for no damn reason other than one foot went in front of the other aimlessly.

Your mind is where it's at.

Use it or lose it.

CHAPTER 67

Still, the Memories

My mother looked into my watery ten-year-old eyes with disgust and told me in a hushed, authoritative tone, "Dry it up and stop causing a scene" (though I had never been so subdued and quiet in my life). She chose to scold me over holding me. I wept quietly and dutifully. The clock ticked as the sun went down. Like it was yesterday, I remember the pain that shot up from my belly through my back from "down there." I was more alone than alone has ever been.

As I write this book, these memories flood out, along with the fears that came with them. I even feel like a child again—the scared one, who was afraid to turn on the overhead lights. I quietly and quite clumsily made my way to the bathroom, holding my aching tummy with only the outside lights highlighting the once beautiful home. These memories have stopped me from writing this book many times.

However, why? Integrity is an interesting thing.

What do you do when no one is looking? That night, for enough time (and it didn't take much), no one was looking. When you write a book, those old places may feel like a prison again. You're not going backwards. To tell the truth, you will have to relive the movements that, ultimately, were life-changing moments many of us were too young to understand.

Loneliness is the real prison. Through that room would forever be the picture I'd see at my darkest moments for the rest of my life.

The feelings I felt when this demon shoved himself into me, stealing my childhood all at once, remain. He stole from me. I swore he was tearing me in half. Would I look the same?

Would I be a mother one day like I always wanted to be? I left my body when these thoughts and worse ones started crashing into me as my head did the headboard.

They would overwhelm me as I tried to tell my story alone for the first time, more than once. I would finally share it openly in front of rooms full of people. Many were crying. Others were indifferent. Most jaws dropped in shock. But you don't look like "that type." What type? The type that was raped? What does that look like? Please tell me.

I no longer have that anger, though ignorance annoys me to my core. Many would rather not know what they don't need to or want to know. However, this story isn't a story. Though it is a tale as old as time, you could say. Uncles and cousins have married each other for centuries. It doesn't make it OK or right.

Women have come so far. However, rape, molestation, incarceration, not feeling heard, are still prevalent. Women are the vessel God choose to give life to all. Yet, we are treated less in every way. I understand not every man has these desires, and most won't act on them. But when they do, more of us should be able to tell you, you, or you, before one life leads to a collision course, killing you and your story from the pain.

CHAPTER 68

Disclaimer: Probably Wasn't Supposed to See That Either

I desperately miss living at Chateau, my home for three months. Yes, these are where my thoughts go some days. I recall moments I didn't cherish that happened too fast. While living in this notorious room, his favorite room from the 60's for three months, I swore I felt his presence. I heard the creaks as I slowly walked a straight line to the balcony that overlooked Sunset Boulevard to my right and the Chateau's tiny windows and old-school, small Euro-style outside sitting area. From my spot, I would inhale the cool, breezy, smog-filled air that I loved every morning. I had to remind myself this was my life. I would perch, ready to write and sip coffee and barely touch my food.

Without a doubt, "Karuna" giggles would echo through the L-shaped structure of the twenty odd floors. I was on the seventh floor. Their place was two balconies over, in accordance with the building's structure. I would listen to the busy streets below. The daily view of the newsstand across the boulevard. Right next door was a coffee shop, one of my favorite places to get green tea ice cream. While thinking and trying to focus on my writing, I'd hear all the noise of the town that's like no other.

My oatmeal, sprinkled with brown sugar and thick maple syrup would remain barely touched. This breakfast room service brought me like clockwork at 10:00 a.m. every morning would include fresh coffee and tons of sparkling water to hydrate myself. Also, like clockwork there they were, "Karuna" and "Edward", her giggling and—what's the saying?—canoodling? Honestly, they were both screwing over their spouses with champagne at 10:00 a.m., and all I thought was, *Fuck, I'm sorry, Damn, reality does bite.*

Sometime later that week, Val was at my door. I was sure he assumed I gave a shit, or worse, I was the press. Not even close. Yet he wanted to hang out. I smiled and kindly shut the door, wondering, *Wtf was "Karuna" Thinking?"* He was sweaty, old, and far too bold. No question mark, my friends. I was straight up not having it.

However, there was no evening I was alone back then. So, I was busy with my man. This was before "me too." But we would all end up at the same place twenty years later for opposite reasons—me, the abused, and them, their abusers—as 2017 Hollywood began to really fall apart. I am clearly all about speaking out your truth, of course, and clearly. But damn it sucked.

But that night—still in my black slip dress and lace panties, because that's what my man liked and was very vocal about—I didn't see the control then. Nor did I see the fact that, when I wasn't well or quite me, he too would disappear. Like I guess Uma did to Val. That night, I was alone and wanted to have someone to talk to too. At barely twenty-one, I was never alone until—and that would remain the case until I would turn thirty-eight. And then forty was when it really changed.

Looking back, I see myself crawling into bed without a care in the world, more worried about the creaks the floor made and if the window would be too noisy while letting in that perfect Septembernight air back home. We spent the night doing many things. Some were sleeping. Others were up on uppers, talking about everything and anything and then falling asleep holding each other. We always were sexual, and he would wake me more than once throughout the night, if my nightmares didn't have me gasping for air and screaming, "Stop," before "he" would lay on my belly and listen to my heart and the growls of lack of nutrition daily howling loud enough, always embarrassing me. He would laugh and order fries, knowing I would eat that.

While we waited, he thought it was fun to make me come before they came. He did, every time. The knock at the door always startled me out of my complete nirvana. I rarely felt complete, except with him or at work in studios. I thought I cherished the times we spent together—during the later '90s and then most of 2000's the most because life was deep in tours and exciting, and we were our own thing. We didn't need to blast it to everyone.

After I left for my kids' sake, I came home regularly throughout the years. We met up every time I came home. Tragically, he has conveniently chosen to shut me out. As I age? Last we spoke in person, he said, "Thank God you look so good. You were the youngest I was with and now the oldest."

I wasn't sure how to take it. Right away, he caught my smile, slowly dull as it sunk into my old skull. He immediately put his phone down. No selfies back then. I had tons of Polaroids that were stolen or destroyed.

Life was simpler, and I wish I would have inhaled and taken it in. But how would I know exactly twenty years later, "he" would be in my aunt's basement apartment, not exactly the Chateau. But we both have lost a lot over the years due to poor choices and the facts of being in the business. Today was also a weekend, a spring Saturday, versus a late September Friday after partying or spending hours in the studio. He came over and picked me up, saying, "You look the same, still in the lace panties and the lace and satin top." He told me I felt the same as he carried me to the bed a mere few feet away.

I suddenly felt nervous and like I shouldn't have brought up age in relation to the book or time in general. The man who I could talk to about anything was still listening, but he noticed I was tense. And we both fought to get back to the passion we'd shared just five years before.

The last time, we'd both still had financially secure and were in a suite at one of the best hotels. Now, we were in my aunt's Hills basement. It was beautiful, though, with a view and lemon trees just outside the windows. I wish I had focused on the moment we were sharing together and not time missed and all the things we'd had to overcome without having each other to text or call. We'd just stopped talking when my daughter got really sick. One had secrets, and one had way too many tricks to keep smiles on faces and spirits up.

Was their marriage over? Or was it typical of Hollywood love? You might have hall passes, depending on whether that's how you roll.

I had one, and my ex knew every time—because I don't lie. I can't live myself if I am consciously choosing to not tell the truth. The fact was this one person is my break, my special place. Or he was. Do I miss him, like I do the melting into my bed at the Chateau, the constant catering to my needs, and our steamed showers in the one modern part of every room, the bathroom? The door had keys like they did in the 1930s.

I wanted everyone to experience my life as much as I was.

CHAPTER 69

My Thoughts Depart Me Sometimes

Now, a decade later, I can just now afford a week there if I wanted to. But it wouldn't be wise. And for what?

After my chill mornings and after "he" would leave before traffic to get over the hill, I started a screenplay in the early 2000's.

It's now my next book. Though it's also true, I have also changed all the names and will tell you the truth as a fiction-based story about three young Hollywood women. I will say one singer is a mix of a Midwestern girl who had to leave after the drugs and rejection were too much. You will realize the only full character is me, watching everything happen around me- during some of my most carefree days.

It was also a time I was watching my friends, including the one I characterized as one girl. Both were singers and had been given plenty of opportunities. One became one the most famous pop stars to this day from that time. I had introduced my Midwestern friend to her and the studio, after hearing her sing at a club a table over. (We had the same birthday, we soon found out.) Like my dad, I heard talent over any noise.

The true character who meshes with her was starting to fall apart at the same time. They both were succumbing to the excesses of Hollywood. I was definitely guilty too. However, I would bounce around for my kids for a few months at times.

Did I understand Hollywood? Yes, It didn't really hit me until I was writing this book. It was a part of me. It was like reading a room of these very judgmental faces staring at me.

Still, by the design of my childhood, I was plenty trained at being two people. That's how I was able to survive life in my house growing up. How I stayed as tough as I could while being hushed. I lived with a lump in my throat.

It's like my thoughts fall from a tree right above my head on a perfect, warm day. I try to catch them in unison and put them where they belong. However, after three weeks of attempting to put these chapters in order, a question has been made obvious to me as I write, and it's obvious to you I am sure: Can this chick just stick with one thought? Well, they run together, as periods of my life have. Memories come through clearly, and then a thought will knock down my brain's door. My thoughts are like my unorganized drawers, where I know exactly where everything is, though it may look like the drawer of a half-assed slob to someone else.

And so, amid a starting point of me at Chateau, hearing giggles o my right and seeing things I wasn't supposed to see or tell you, to my left, I'm watching "him" turn toward the Valley side of the Sunset, heading to the studio after a shower. I was young and trauma bent still. I was lost and have become more found than I knew was even possible. I didn't, until I was framed so easily on a set by choosing not to use dope with a lead the night before we filmed early the next morning.

Though this isn't methodically written, these memories triggered do round back to where I was.

Damn, life happens so fast in that town.

Today, I am sad it isn't the same as Hollywood I grew up around and began working in. Still, I have words and the memories of the people, places, and things on these pages. It's a just story about a time, a girl, some loves, some heartbreak, with scenery in between and healing (even though I am a little *bossy*, in all caps, sometimes).

I spent too many years pretending I got this, blaming myself and others for not finishing anything I started or, in essence, giving up.

What I really did was walk away to other beautiful lives with those I love, and I'm still alive to tell you about it.

When I would be on my balcony with wet hair, writing what will be my second publication, I would watch the world I love unfold, not realizing that day would be so far away decades later. Don't let time get away from you. Don't waste time on anyone who doesn't see you, worse doesn't see past beauty.

Except one truth—we are loved and worthy. And my thoughts fall off my brain's branches into places that seem to not match. There is no right way to remember your life. I am curious how much longer this will take. I can't tell you everything. Even though I am only forty-one this month, I have lived many lives. And hopefully you will relate to parts of these messy markers in time.

Please don't make the same mistakes I did. Love and money with unhealed pain can lead to a collision course as brutal as being abused at work or at home—and to a life that looks different than it could've been. Focus on the things we have in common. We all want love, to be loved, to be understood, and to be healed from pain. I can't make any promises, but I can say love is an enigma.

So, why not love the fuck out of ourselves? Because when you do, you won't care when he drives away. And you won't ask yourself if you made the right impression the next time you meet someone you like. Just be you, without worrying what happens next. No one is a prize to everyone. We are all trying to figure it out, and most are in disguise. What if I had I known then—while I was sitting on my terrace trying to let go of all that baggage I hadn't even faced—what I know now?

We have to face it.

What comes to mind?

What do you have to face?

CHAPTER 70

My Mezzo Mix Mind

The last time my mother and I spoke, I was getting a brain scan to make sure I'd healed from drug use. I was told by doctors just last November my brain scan results proved no problems. Nor was there evidence of the mental illness that always pinned on me my whole life. That was my first taste of freedom, finally. I thought touring or love had been. But no, it was knowing I was a highly functional human being who suffered from severe and very, very old PTSD caused by my childhood trauma only.

By the end of this book, you will know who I am and those who I am grateful for—now or before. We all have moments, and few, if any, last forever. But hating yourself over someone else's actions is not your part ever to play.

This book is about a lot. It's about life clearly, but it's about honesty and freedom mostly. For a while, I lost myself. We all do. Many times, I felt sure I'd forgotten how to be a badass until my daughter's cancer diagnosis. Almost losing a child could have taken me down. But I went into beast mode and advocated for my baby girl. It's not only my job, it was natural, even through my shock and inconsolable pain for her.

Some days, it consumed me and almost took me down. Her strength was empowering. I am proud of her strength. I gave her all I had when she was sick, as I should. But when her cancer was "gone," a few days later, I realized, so was I. How would I turn the volume back up in my mind and light the fire back up in my belly? Would this be the question?

Or was this just more doctors wondering why I was writing so much. I am a writer, and someone is listening to trauma. So why not give you the parts that made me, me. But the part right before she gets her powers? I had those for twenty years. Three years ago, I had a baby, a boy, and was joyful.

Bear with me as I strip down to my bare bones with you watching my thoughts—as I untie the dress, or unbutton my jeans, depending on where I have been the day I tell you more about my life and my days. My thoughts, like my style, are riddled with rips and rhymes. I repeat myself and forget I told you that last time. The memories aren't methodically pouring out. They come more like a mezzo mix of every soda at the quick trip, all mixed. Repetition is what we need, but it sucks and bores my brain—and actually my muscles too. So let's get through this together, and if you made it past the moments that may have shocked you, thank you.

You may have more questions than answers, and I may bore you.

I may make you want more. I don't know. I just can't get any older without freeing you and me.

Are you asking yourself, *What is this all for?* This is for letting go. This is about more than my words. Hopefully, parts of my story take you back, and the many mantras I stowed in these paragraphs will bring closure to your very own pain.

CHAPTER 71

Perfection Isn't Reality

After my rape, I acted out in school. I had stomach pains and slept a lot or not enough. I couldn't concentrate. Nor did I participate in classes like I had before. I began carving "perfection isn't reality" on every desk I sat in. Then I was introduced to tagging in eighth grade, and that became my calling card. That was when the journalism teacher asked me to be an editor and writer for the school paper. I remember the way she looked at me. It was now a few years later, and my behavior had worsened, though I wasn't mean or unkind. I was just lacking my highest potential, purposely. What was the point? The way she looked at me, it was like she saw through me. She requested that I talk to someone if I had no one at home who was listening. My writing gave away the depth of my pain.

I tried to erase my pain on paper. If I got carried away, I'd start telling a story. Or I'd mention the lamp I carried with pain in places I never felt, and maybe this plug would be a way to electrocute me. I shocked myself with that thought three years later in one of my favorite classes, creative writing and drama. By high school, it would be a debate I loved. I was a great speaker after I had been silenced. In debate and writing, I felt empowered.

I am truly grateful today, there are resources for you with the internet, I didn't have. You can courageously look up what happened to you. Don't be afraid of the answer; others' reactions; or, worse, your lack of reaction if you were raped or abused (shaken up by your very own experience outside of your control). There is no right way to handle such brutality. Remember, if your experience left you feeling afraid, in pain, confused, angry, or at a loss for a description or where to begin because of denial by others and yourself—that's what kept me quiet for twenty-four years. I get it.

CHAPTER 72

We All Want to Overcome

We all are able to overcome fears, even after severe trauma. However, what about the in between moments in? We want to be lions, right? I am sitting up in bed listening to a motivational speaker I love. Always wanting to discover more of who I am, not was. Telling the truth and being kind are the most valuable virtues in life. I teach my children these virtues today as much as they will listen. This book is about the past leading to the present.

I felt fearless back in my 20s, And I had a job in Lethal Dose studio for the next two years. Of course, I hadn't had any trauma healing yet, so I ruined it, And horribly. I started like a lion. And until I was in a constant healing state, I either didn't finish it by not going back, or worse, I was kicked out and wasn't spoken to again. It was brutal. However, it was my fault.

Sick people can easily make others sick or feel sick, feel off. People throughout my life have loved quickly and given me the key to their safes, both hypothetically and actually. However, my intensity would become too much. Though my intentions were honest, and I was open, sometimes being too open is a turnoff. Staying self-aware and being able to read the room are basically the same thing. Being self-aware will change all your relationships for the positive.

Did I make another U-turn? Y'all, that is my life. A bunch of crazy shit has happened. And I am trying to organize it all. I'm going on my fourth trip home to the Hills to write. I am most inspired there, as that was where I truly became me. The moment I landed in 1996 at fifteen, I knew this was my home. Little did I know what was about to happen soon after. My life would become one most would dream of. However, enjoying it and cherishing each moment was not a part of my daily hygiene. My friends, your daily hygiene should be completely and totally about cherishing yourself first and each moment you are invited into. You will realize you do have a place in this world, even after severe trauma, addiction, depression, and anything else that has held you back. Whatever it was, it will dissipate over time.

I remember when it actually clicked. The same day, I lost it and someone I will always miss.

Chapter 73

Time's a Damn Thief

My kids understand and are excited that Mommy is Mommy again. They had heard of that fearless girl who became a mom. Now, they will see me on *Magazine* covers and as an author and never stopping or giving up regardless. Listen, Moms, we know we are superheroes. But to our kids, we are their version. I wish we all just got it. However, I was either great or horrible at everything I did my whole life. That includes motherhood. My oldest daughter—a gorgeous, intelligent, driven college student, who at six foot two is modeling and is the taller version of me—is extremely distant from me right now. In truth, 90 percent of the time was being away from her, and the rest was being physically hooked. There was no making it anymore. It didn't matter what I accomplished; it was never enough. I didn't know what I was doing and what for. I always wanted to work in the industry. I never said this role is exactly me. I'll never forget and this is why I am still trusted by many in the business (though some might only be picking up this book to see if they're in it or make sure they aren't). If any of you wonder what secrets I will tell, then you don't know me at all.

There's one thing about home I didn't realize until a few years ago (and it pisses me off how blind I was). This town, this Hollywood, is extremely segregated as recently as…umm, still now. We unpack fame in this book, and somewhat devalue it. Sorry. However, the lies that surround it are robbing many people of their courage to step out. Too many are comparing themselves to other *humans*. *The difference is determination*!

Every day was like a show. I always felt like I was in a reality show—before they even existed. People tell me today, if your life had been recorded from the late '90s through 2007 (holy shit, truth), it would be a watch-worthy show. Sometimes, it would be a shit show. But every single day, there was something happening around me with people you're now watching on TV. I still don't know how I got there. I don't know how those ten years were so insane, and I was right in the middle of it all. However, just like with everything, what goes up must come down—worse, if you used your looks and only half your brain. Now, at forty, I feel lost a lot. So when I was asked for the twelfth time to write a book, it was time.

I should high-five myself for just being here. The truth is not everyone will like this book. Many won't find it helpful. Many of you will think this is a story of Hollywood alone. It was my home for many years' that's where my memories and messes were mostly made.

I still pay a high price just to go home and give my kids the happy life of the valley.

CHAPTER 74

Breathless

I remember the first time I woke up breathless. Like you always hear, the past comes back to haunt you. Yes, it's true. One day, out of nowhere it all hits at once. Now in my thirties, my kids are half-grown. Look over at the one of three who stayed. Looking closely, you wonder if he was the one you were supposed to marry. Or were you pleasing others again? Were you searching for safety again? That day, you wake up and realize you wasted more time, running from the scene of a crime you didn't commit. I was thirty-two when it all hit. How old were you? That is why I am screaming from my bed in my house, tucked away in suburbia—the kind with neighbors who ring the damn doorbell.

(I hate that shit. Text first—*dayummm*.)

Forgive me, but, there will be many interruptions in time throughout this book. Why? My life, like the night, is still youngish. OK, it's 3:00 p.m., and I already took something for my head.

Almost everything has made me miss LA, or the life I left rather. The neighbors are kid, and only want to welcome me. Only then it becomes every fucking holiday and all their kids birthdays too?

Fuck, it's a different kind of hell, only because I wasn't brought up right...to even finish that sentence at all. Expect the unexpected, sure. But not to be all la-di-da.

I do ask God, When did it first happen? When I didn't want to deal with, umm, people? Jesus, how many hells? What I have learned is that we're all smiling. Why? How many of us are hiding? Is your pain as annoying, especially when you're bored, like mine?

Chapter 75

Dizzy and Ugly in Times Square

The ugly truth hit me in New York City. It was at Times Square, one of the busiest places there is. I was in my early twenties. I had been on my first cover of an international magazine. So, even though I was barely five eight, business was booming. I was on the way to an audition—back when casting directors' stares alone would telepathically tell a girl to get a nose job and then come back. (So many girls ran off crying, and the guy with the "cool" version of fake Prada glasses would get to me.) It was always the same. "You're booked, but if you were taller, you'd be in Milan with that face."

Back to the memory that almost had me—lose it I mean. Being a mother saved me time and time again. Like a painting I am staring at, vividly, I float into my memories. I am nauseous a lot. My ex-husband and best friend tells me I put too much pressure on myself.

I reply, "I'm a fucking hamster on a wheel going nowhere."

He looks at me knowingly. Also, his biggest fear is that I am going somewhere.

I was a disappointment to many, when I would lose my way— He tried to listen to the counselors and turn me away. But he couldn't. Maybe it was my daughters in unison looking through the blinds. *Those are my kids*. Tears rolled down my face.

While the world was fucked and I had a story to tell. Then when I came to, I'd call my agent. He had known me since I was almost seventeen. I lived in a model apartment off and on. My ex infiltrated that relationship too. Surprising me but not him. He would send me to his best clients. I could sell ice to Eskimos, he would say. He wanted me to be an actress. However, like anything else, I fucked it up.

Studios aren't as forgiving I would find out. This isn't improv, Brooklin. I couldn't help it. Some scripts made us women sound stupid. So I would improvise, and eventually I'd get fired. I was never good at following rules or running with the herd. Shutting up has never been a characteristic. It was a trait I wasn't born with and never learned. Taming me, ALMOST impossible. Fuck, I gotta pee again. (Mom life)

Back to that memory, my brain insists we run through, like a script. Don't miss your cue, Brooklin. There I was. OK that just sounds fucked up, and it was the same way everyone else started. It's true, and I was dizzy but standing still. Boring! I felt so alone. (Suck me off, twenty-two-year-old me; you're annoying.) Still it's true. It may have happened to you. People were passing by, some knocking into me, but I was in my own world. I was feeling everything I had ever felt in that moment—in less than a minute. That was the first time I'd realized life was passing me by.

When the past really began haunting me, was the moment my daughter was born.

A year before, But when my daughter was born, it all changed. You see, my mother approved of this pregnancy. How can you love someone so much in one second? I knew I would kill anyone who hurt this child of mine. My baby, the moment I laid eyes on her, my baby girl. That is when the hate and confusion for my mother came back full force, sending me into what they called postpartum depression. It was deeper, it was my trauma resurfacing and, soon, taking over.

But first, My mother peeked around the corner. I know meeting her grand baby changed her. To this day my Mother is a decent grandmother. Maybe she regrets what she didn't do for my sister, brother, or me. I watched my mother gazing at my baby with such love. She was holding her awkwardly, though, like she had never had babies of her own. Weird, my ex and I thought.

Since she was born, my daughter has been my obsession. All my kids would be and are. The same big blue eyes as mine stare back each time I look at them. My first daughter was different. She knew something. Maybe what Mommy was going through? I'm not exactly sure. But my first words after she was given to me were, "She knows more than me." She is so intelligent and intense. She is like her Mother whether she likes it or not.

Now at twenty-one and in college. Back then, I nursed her for two years and took her everywhere, including work trips—like this one, a memory so vivid, as I said earlier. However, I allowed life to go on, pushing my daughter swiftly through the huge crowd. She was in the best stroller money could buy. That was another lesson I would learn. Money doesn't buy happiness. Nor does it last if you're trying to buy a life you don't need. If it's built on money, it isn't yours. Having money isn't the problem. Building a life solely based on it is. I know because I did it for years. The world is fucked. How you are forgotten when you can't rent a private plane anymore or be the one who pays someone's rent. Suddenly, you are nothing.

To my little girl, I was everything, and she was a giggly, happy child. I loved watching her toddle around, running to me for the millionth hugs that day. Yet, still, thank God I knew she saw the world differently—not like me. Another day, I'd choose again to bury it all and keep moving forward. Toward?

CHAPTER 76

Three Ice Cubes and Water

The sign shut off that day. The word *failure* was flashing less than it had yesterday. It was still there, though, in neon green. It accompanied the compulsive thought always plaguing me, running a marathon in my head. *You will fail, and no one will care.*

I walked past the lemon trees and didn't look back as I heard him pass me swiftly. Nothing was said out the window, nothing. I kept staring at the juicy lemons and told myself, *I am still full of so much.*

I am just cutting myself open. And the juice that pours out may sting your eyes from the truth. Add sugar and let me pour myself into a cup with three ice cubes so the lemonade I just made won't splash your eyes. You said that's why I need to use three ice cubes. So I will listen to you as usual. And as I pour my truth in that cup, I know you will cautiously look at me thinking, *Shit, why am I here again? She means nothing. She is crazy.* As you drink. You see the truth—the cliché of a girl who has grown up and never judged you or anyone. Yet, I have been judged by everyone who I won't fuck or all the groupies who hated me for being the only girl in the crew.

That's just the surface. What plagues me is, while I watch you drink still, I walk away and force myself to not give a shit if you pay attention to the truth or not. This isn't just one person. This is about all the names in neon lights I supported and loved, who I kept secret and sealed like a juicy, overripe lemon. I was too kind. I took no credit for anything. I was weak. and I am paying for it now. My life has been blessed, but as I watch most of my former friends on the big screen or DJ-ing or even on stages, there is one who makes me the most upset. Look and he is not standing; he can't sit still.

Even if this moment was more real than what I wish had happened, it's true. He wanted water and me that day and left and never came back. He has called me trash and other horrible things. It stands for what is happening in you if you drink from what I pour. You may well treat women better. Remember who has stood by you through years. Regardless of our own trials apart, we live fast lives and keep busy. I don't know why I never came home as you asked me every time we spoke until, one day, some random person told you lies. And I am not the most sour lemon you ever had.

Almost the same neon signs kept us higher than we should have been. It all ends with me saying I was your youngest and now your oldest. Shitty neon lights out. I'm still just under two decades younger and was once that town's little prize. I fucked up and saw the love in your's and others eyes, especially YOUR dark pools... I believed weren't lies.

I picked up the cup you finished after you left, tossing a fresh lemon I'd just picked when you passed me by with little or no goodbye. If it wasn't for a glass of wine with a friend, I would have cried, because I realized it was over. I made it worse with my outbursts and trying to make it right. My intense mind was confused, no longer seeing you and others in bright lights—now that we have aged, including me, the youngest in the crew back then.

I was the only girl Lethal Dose let work in his studio and trusted with all the messes that had to be cleaned up and never spoken of. Hollywood is nothing like what anyone thinks. Take what you assume is happening behind closed doors and multiply it by a thousand. That sucks when I just want to be normal, after all these years. But everyone I have been back in touch with is having a midlife crisis and, with me turning forty, literally had me ghosted.

The further I go, or rather the more I type, it fades. As I move toward somewhere, at the end, the sign's completely gone. The more

I power through, the more the sign starts falling. Is it the wind or my dedication?

I can say with assuredness, the worst place a mind can go is comparing ourselves to anything or others at all. It's technically impossible because we're all our very own *person*. The devil's playground is our mind, telling us a different story. Knowing this, our realities should never be the same, but we go on comparing all the same—feeling shame. We are wasting so much time pretending, when we're perfectly and wonderfully made. Drink up. No need to make someone drink you; that's lame of me to tell that story. Ugh!

They have gotten too much attention in this book—though it was decades, and true. I just want to delete half the shit I wrote before I got here—when the neon sign came crashing down.

It doesn't *not* hurt. Letting go sucks. But we have to care enough for ourselves to stop wondering why they don't. Then one pops back up and asks,

"When are you coming home?"

I have picked people to be my homes, rather than my very own place. And now I am forty and fighting for my life, not to ever need anyone. That's my ultimate goal.

What's your ultimate goal?

CHAPTER 77

Rape Is a Strong Word, and So Is God to Some

Rape is a strong word, but it should be heard. I have accepted my mother, after years of manipulation and guilt-tripping her. The truth is, she's still in denial.

By thirteen, when I finally began to turn pain into hard work, my life began to change. First, of course, for a good ten years, I had to compartmentalize—like putting a book on a shelf. So that's what happened. I focused on dancing, and that victory will be told. Your dreams can still come true.

Sometimes I would look at my mother when she wondered why I skipped class or was being a smart-ass. I would want to scream, "You walked in while your child was being…"

She started to realize I was about to bust and, now, a teen and pregnant. She had to get rid of me. Finally, when I was fifteen years old, neither of us could look at each other, and she sent me away.

The trauma would rear its ugly head for years off and on. However, I didn't talk about what had happened to me for thirteen years. However, during that time, I used my pain for gain and accomplished four of my dreams and now this one. I refused to let it stop me, and that makes some think it wasn't so bad. No, ya fuck, life goes on, and this world chooses to ignore anyone hurting—like my mother did. I had to get away from her. For a year, I still trained in dance.

I guess, I needed a big dose of *rape* to get away and meet my dad and be a little badass, as my dad calls me.

By seventeen, I was on a stage in front of thousands of people on the most popular music tour of the late '90s and early 2000s. Certain things and types of people still trigger me. I am disgusted by my abuser and despise my mother. I hadn't had much stability, so relationships have been hard for me. I have loved the same two men for over twenty-three years and one other in between. Because of this book, I lost one. I am quite intense.

People hold shame and blame differently. But today, as a mother, I can't fathom not choosing my child to protect, choosing instead to hush and seemingly resent my own child. The choice I made was to make my mother pay—which wasn't my best choice in life. I was almost eleven, and I was hurt and angry.

This did, however, change everything. It finally got me out of that place and my life.

Yet, I am still the one he chose to ruin.

I look back now, and I think, *Dude, I was only ten years old.*

Then my memories go back to soaked sheets and my long dark hair stuck to half my face by the tears and his sweat. As my mom finally flew in after hearing my one loud shocking screech, I slowly turned my head. I can honestly tell you my fearful thoughts at that very moment. *Am I lost? You're here.*

Then my next memory—she wasn't there for me. She was there for her.

As a mother now, the forgiveness, or lack thereof, eats me up. I type this word for word. After five years of hell, much caused by anger, I was sent to my older sister's.

I flew to Hollywood, and my life changed.

Things happen in life. Hold on. You never know what God is about to send you. Go with it if your God gut is calm. I was too young when I began a relationship with a famous musician.

Dave Weiderman, who became my dad, saved my life. He happened to be a famous producer. He was there to push me to make all my dreams realized, yet he made me work for them. I had to audition for everything I did. I hope anyone hurting knows this: *Your pain will lead you to a destiny you can't even imagine.* Pain has a way of making you stronger and more empathetic, though you'll be afraid at first. Many of us love hard or not at all. Finding balance after severe trauma will be the hardest part of life. We don't want anyone hurt like we have been. Our kindness is mistaken for weakness, or mine was. Your vindication is coming. Choose to believe you deserve to be wined and dined.

Trauma is all the same. After pain and shame, you are stronger and wiser. Tell yourself this: *Those who hurt me are sick, and it's not my fault.* This is my life and the truth. It wasn't all her fault. My mother is like an old overwork pair of designer shoes; she overstays her welcome, every time. She lets everything go. I keep getting torn between the strong me today and the moment I dramatically turned my head, a child who knew I wasn't somehow anymore. That night became the turning point of my entire life. She never came back. The clock ticked; tears silently ran down my face. I yelled, "Please stop." I couldn't hear my tears, so no one did. So, stop!

Saturday Morning, I smelled bacon, and I finally was so hungry I came out. I heard my mother laughing without a care. So that was it. I was supposed to be me from yesterday. But that girl was dead.

Looking behind me, as I was throwing on cutoffs, my tan legs seemed different. My long dark hair seemed different. I looked in the mirror. My eyes were brighter. I was more aware, though still afraid. I made a choice right then—not fear; I will make this shit my power. I lay alone in that room, thinking, *This is my body.* My life had been torn in half by an old man's devious decision. That bed, soaked by tears, and the posters on the walls were the only ones who saw the whole truth. I knew it was no longer about laughing and love. I was now merely surviving.

Looking back now, I know why he chose me. My mom was neglectful, and she was bought off easily. This may upset people. So may my story. The truth hurts. But I won't ever lay in silence or fear again. So many need healing—before they make the mistakes I ended up making.

I wish I knew exactly what to say—what you all need to hear. Hopefully, knowing pain is pain and you are not alone will help. You're so worthy. I know nothing about how to write a book, but I'm here. The cold sweats and glimpses from the past will never fully stop. But numbing them with drugs doesn't stop it either.

I hate staying in this place too long. So let's move on to the dirty shit unhealed trauma turns into—loveless love, addiction, trying too hard or not enough, getting addicted to something or a few someones. The latter has been my biggest addiction, despite years and years fighting with heroin.

Still, a lot happened between then and now.

CHAPTER 78

Hollywood: The Smallest Circle

Many have asked for years. You won't tell the secrets of Hollywood. Those hills are filled with moments that live in the darkness of night, ending at dawn. I was there for much of two decades, right in the middle. The smallest circle I've ever known is Hollywood. We are only there by blood, fame, or marriage, plus the occasional outsider. When I say occasional, I mean even a childhood friend had to be given a confidentiality paper to sign. I ran into "Ashton" at Jamba Juice at noon, less than six hours after he was squinting while happily impaired; we were at a regular exclusive party.

Now years later, I realize staying determined after forty is a superpower. In our twenties, nothing seemed to matter. I used his name because he probably hasn't changed from his Middle America upbringing. However, still he winked and waved. We didn't talk until we saw each other again. It was another Hollywood Night, a bunch of us misfits at a VIP table. It mattered then, but nothing lasts forever. I've mentioned that, haven't I? However, Hollywood like me, beats to its own drum.

Does losing friends hurt?
Or does losing love hurt worse?

CHAPTER 79

Truth's the Best Motivator

I had just finished my third national tour as a dancer. had his almost career-ending injury. I was still dancing pro, locally. Carmen headlined as a Doll at the Viper Room on Sunset. We had Chris, Gwen and others over the years. I was dancing chorus three nights a week on Sunset. This was before my addiction and after my first tours. I skipped around from tours, industry work, relationships.

Being overcomers (you, too, friends) from different traumas (which is my point), we are gripping our adrenaline to become more involved in the system. I'm working my way toward forensic psychology, and Kim, a lawyer. We both have experienced things most Hollywood "wealthy" kids don't. Or maybe we're unafraid to be of help and honest about our own mistakes. Let's not operate in *shame*. Truth is motivation.

My point of this story is for the purpose of establishing that no one's life is perfect, and we all have dreams and aspirations that don't always come easily. However, don't quit. I promise you that dream will happen or become a better one along the way—because you did the next right thing.

CHAPTER 80

Looking Back at the Past I Miss

I can't stand the reality of the past sometimes—that it is the past, even, that it's over. Every detail may not be what you remember. However, it is what I saw and experienced. Many want to know all the exciting things. I whined to a friend from the highest of days recently, saying, "It was getting weird or it was already." He agreed I was getting weirder. But he also agreed this book would be good for me.

How much do others remember of the things that meant so much to me? Do you feel like that? Few will fully get you. Fewer will feel the same way you do at any given time. What I loved about performing, particularly touring as a dancer, is the energy. All our energy before performances was the same. We were all buzzing—some organically and others, shaky but still stoked and feeling it. That was me sometimes. Don't laugh. You'd be nervous, too, at seventeen in this whole new world.

Some nights, I would shake and Fred would say as he made his way upstage, "You know what time it is?"

I'd then hear his voice echoing through the arena hallway—his deeper stage voice. It pumped us up no doubt. That was our cue to get in places. We were right behind him in a row, though if shifted, I was always directly behind Fred. He was super supportive.

I'd hit that stage and suddenly become some else. When on stage, I became stronger than I had ever been. I had made it to where I wanted to be. Though it lasted for a while, All must come to an end. I held dear many people with whom I shared those times and years with. Some I kept in touch with for many years. Some have passed. Others I talk to today. Yes, there was "him," who I thought I loved. I was young. He was on tour. He was lead in another band. In fact, two men I would spend significant time with (one of whom I'd live with) were on that tour. We were our own world back then.

I knew I was running even then. However, I was still running in the right direction. No dope yet. I really was in a world I had dreamt of. Each would end after three to twelve weeks, depending on a number of factors.

In between, I was given the job at Lethal Dose Studio. I spent two years answering phones; cleaning up; and hiding people from the paparazzi, as we were across from Hollywood. What became my favorite task was kicking out idiots. Le would look at me, and I knew. He was very intense at work. We would let loose every two weeks at most. Those nights were fun. The clean-up wasn't.

I was to pick the girls who could come in. That was easy, as I had beautiful friends. Courtney, a model with mocha skin and green eyes and is one of my best friends to this day. She was in the studio almost every night with me. There were a few more. But she was a regular.

These were some of the best years of my life—so much so I have spent thousands going home to Hollywood to write this book. Everyone has changed. I saw a few from then. "Pep" is doing really well; he's a renowned photographer today. Most are still always in studios twenty years later. Many are still touring. Though the tours are smaller, they are still going strong. There are Seth and others whose friendships I value.

However, I had to be told to snap out of my 20s.

Writing this book got me stuck for sure. One of the most common symptoms of unhealed trauma is self-sabotage (and not the group or song). Within two amazing years, I found a way to sabotage the best job I have had to this day (and I wish I had listened to Le more while I had it.) I was only twenty-two, but I threw away the best years. How? Drugs, continuing to date a rocker—one who was almost twenty years older than me.

I was warned by Lethal Dose. And one day he changed the locks and wouldn't let me into the studio, my life. It felt over. I did it though, and with warning and constant changes. He said over the cameras I knew faced me, "Go to rehab." Within a week, I did.

Those who had relationships stayed in touch. Hollywood can be fickle, as well as fame. I keep in touch with five or six people from the whole crew. All the friends I made have scattered across the United States, and many became famous—some whose rent I paid or who I let live in my penthouse rent free. Like *Breaking Bad*, we've all made mistakes and grown from them—and have broken up ourselves.

After six years of a wild, loud, busy, and exciting life, it became quiet. Many careers in the industry end abruptly. This was before social media. Since social media, many of us have gotten back in touch. However, as I mentioned, the world is sadly still fickle. And so are those who buy into it or earn it. Sadly, some forget where they come from. Many who have our people I met in my teens, and I know exactly where they came from.

Then there are many who have stayed close to my dad and me, have coffee and a chat. People always ask who came into my dad's office the most. That's easy. It was Hudson for sure. Hudson did a lot for the GC and GC lessons and truly would jump into whatever new idea Dad had.

Writing this book took me back. I know I drove Fred and others crazy. Thank you for blessing this book and our memories. Those were some of the best years of all of our lives. A world of its own. Trying to figure out how to explain it hasn't been easy. My memories are a lot.

Those were simpler days, filled with talks with Fred and many others, being nervous before a show, and us girls loving every second. Even showers in arenas and sleeping in vans (no, not the shoes) was fun. Nothing was glamorous about it. But damn, it was a rush. I was a mother in this atmosphere.

I took "Raquel" to my dad's office during the day, and he loved her running around. She was spoiled by rock stars. She just didn't realize it.

Eventually, the fairy tale fell apart.

The paparazzi back then were crazy, and I was a decoy for many. It was how Leo and I became good friends back then. We all had Escalades or Range Rovers, and my penthouse was blocks away. So, we drove together or snuck out of the popular parties back then. All were promoted by specific promoters and special private invites. The parties were at different places almost every night. Unless invited, you wouldn't know where.

There was a code, and tourists would never know where to go—funny because we were not far from the strip.

Life without my children made me do worse. However, within four months, I couldn't take it and went to them. I know many women who won't leave Hollywood. Years pass knowing a career is no longer an option, yet they hope to meet a rich producer, while their mom or grandma has their child or children across the country. I don't agree with it personally. However, I do understand the pull of Hollywood.

I have moved back many times since my teens. I worked for my father. However, as I said before, I had so much trauma. I never spoke of it until my 30s. I kept relapsing over the nightmares and feeling worthless or just not wanting to feel at all. Until Inwas finally done at 33.

We need Trauma Anonymous. Just saying.

You can't compare trauma. Trauma hurts, right? Right. All trauma is in the same part of the brain. And finally, trauma is fucking trauma, and it affects us.

We have to stop making those hurting feel they shouldn't be because it wasn't as bad as what I went through. I have been guilty of comparing, even with my own daughter. She has been quite angry with me.

Do I miss Hollywood? All the time.

But it isn't the same as the "Hills" I grew up in. I'm a '90s kid, and my crew was all over Hollywood or in one of the studios I worked in.

My days are quieter, as my phone isn't buzzing as often. Or I don't wake up to a kind text or a crazy text (sent when he was obviously exhausted from being in the studio all night). For almost two weeks, there's been silence. So now that noise is gone. It did feel like another end again.

But that's what happens. What did it mean? I could have asked myself. However, my friend "Pep" has helped me greatly; I'm learning how to promote myself and do all the things I did for others but not for myself and this book until he reminded me. I am the only one who can do me right. He said, "It's your turn." So that is what I prefer to tell myself. I am still in my prime. I tell myself.

The only unconditional love, because of the God of my understanding. hadn't gotten so addicted. I know that, and they know that. I used to believe I should be judged. *I fucked up my life*, I would think. I didn't. I allowed pain to go deeper and deeper, until my tummy always hurt or the lump in my throat might burst. Instead of talking about my abuse. I used dope to numb it. Please talk about it. Those closest to me didn't believe me or chose to ignore my situation; they indeed knew what happened. We have resources now.

I'm writing this book for anyone who relates and wants to accomplish their dreams. But pain keeps us from moving forward or causes us many symptoms, all leading to the same place—feeling alone, fearful, or fearless if you need noise. Please stop thinking everyone knows and feeling crazy. You are magic. You are strong. You are loved. And you have a whole world waiting for you.

Remember this: There is a place for everyone at the table.

CHAPTER 81

Daddy Squared

I remember when Dad became quicker to introduce me as his daughter Brooklin. Life happened fast with Daddy. He had inductions to the RockWalk. He felt music needed its own place in this crazy town we'd both migrated to. When Dave Weiderman says he's gonna do something, he not only does it, his grand ideas seem to elude the less visionary. They never did me. I saw the same way he did. It was just more proof he was my dad.

Dad is always kind and faithful to my needs, and he always gives to others too. He is greatly loved by everyone. He happened to be one of the biggest names in music. I didn't know this fact at first. It wasn't until my time-outs in his office, when I missed curfew or relapsed, that I learned that.

We spoke upfront about my addiction. He only does the truth, even if it will hurt. "Truth sets you free, Brooklin", he says to this day.

He spent much of his free time helping the community with charities he started or joined.

He'd take me to studios. I'd listen to demos and was trusted to pick what would possibly be popular. Dad gave, gave, and provided a direct route from point A to B.

He included me in his choices for yearly inductions. Yes, I have been known to beg for certain bands. Two bands I had been on tour with and knew needed to be inducted.

Over the year, my time-outs weren't your typical ones; they were even fun. I mean, you never knew who would show up in dad's office. Yet, like everything, All came to an abrupt end.

From the day I met my dad and realized what he did and, over time, who he was, I wanted to learn and grow, not just twiddle my thumbs and be a spoiled little girl. "Good," he would say, "I will spoil you only with love, experience, trust you earn, knowledge, the company we keep, and the excitement. You will become who you already are."

He always said, "Everyone is someone. Never look down on anyone. We are where we are supposed to be, and one day it will make sense. If it doesn't, you aren't paying attention to your own feet."

We all have destiny and a path. I had mine, even when I would interrupt it with one of my addictions, love, pregnancies, and even worse, by my not realizing what a thief time is. I thought my dad would always be the center of it all, not just figuratively but also literally. His office was in the middle of Hollywood, blocks from my entertainment agency; my first place; and plenty of friends throughout the Hills, including his house in the Hills, in a cul-de-sac on the Valley side. He preferred the Valley for family and music studios, though they were freckled across noho over the hill. To this day the best deep breaths I have ever had were while taking in smoggy views from the hills I lived in.

An old friend and I agreed that everywhere else is boring compared to the Hills. We will take the smog over the benefits to our health to stay there forever. When he said it, though, I couldn't keep a straight face. I looked away giggling. Out my kitchen window from my basement apartment was the quintessential Hills view. Even from the basement, I could see the lemons dropping in front of the window, the midmorning sun giving the fat, juicy yellow fruit an orange tint against the equally fresh green avocados, leaning hard and deeper to the ground.

I said, "My son will love just walking outside and picking out his avocado for breakfast.

"He" half listened, going on to explain something about needing water with three ice cubes. Scooting around me, he moaned as all six foot six of him folded back up. He had somehow whirled me around or snuck around me, going for the first kiss we had shared in five years. It was our longest time ever apart. He asked me when I was coming home as he set the water down to pick me up. I knew him well, so I knew he was low enough to see his favorite lace panties and the tattoo on the back of my thigh I knew would make him moan. I can't tell you how he ended up in front of me as he went from my lips to my eyes to his actual height. During that time, I had tucked my long lacey tank into the tip of my panties. He kept explaining softly in his Valley voice about how three ice cubes keeps it from splashing when it pops (I repeated pop while looking in his eyes. now on his hips) "in an uncold drink."

Then he backed up and said, "Can you bring that with us over here?"

I could have teased, "Where?" But I was still calm and at ease and knew not to overthink or speak. Just flow, like he taught me decades ago. Either way, we were always a scene out of a Jackie Collins book. I remember reading them in my late teens and twenties, and I needed to jump his bones. He loved it then. I was eighteen years old, naive, and feeling like the only one. I was for a while, but I doubt as long as I assumed.

I always loved his little drops of wisdom. I, of course, interrupted with my need for three because I like odd numbers. I was half joking, and his dark brown eyes, one with the yellow dot, were even more expressive in the sunlight shining through the hills, avocados, and lemon trees. *What a beautiful man*, I thought.

Then he said, "Oh no, Brooklin. Don't get weird."

And I snapped out of the days he was more a part of me. I realized, first fuck up; today, I was lucky he was even here. He has always been in the studio. It was there when things blossomed most into what almost was more times than he cares to remember. The less I count, the easier it is to remain less angry at myself for running away from it all because of something that happened to me before I had the stability my dad, he, and (by now) my ex were providing.

Besides my dad, I have loved three men, each differently but truly. All three were in the industry and somehow had a mutual friend here and there. However, it turns out I knew everyone, so I was the common denominator for most. I just didn't know it, as I was too busy trying to be enough for something or someone or pretending my life was normal.

It took me a good year to realize who my dad really was—that Dave Weiderman was "the man." He was the fixer, the mixer, and the person everyone went to for advice, as much as his generous freebies from his music store. He is still the most popular. However, since his retirement from the franchise, it has been cut in half. I am partial and will add pictures of his awards of his creations on my website. Dad gave musicians a place of their own, he also made rock and its memorabilia a theme. You can guess which store I'm referring to?

My grandfather started the design in Chicago and then Las Vegas. But it was my dad who retired from playing drums after a bad car accident and without skipping a beat or dwelling on missing the days. And by the time I was in his life for good, we were in PR as well—which, it became obvious, was where I belonged. That was one thing you could trust me with, after the hundreds of coffee orders and at least fifty something unpublished band reviews for the store's exclusive magazine. Yes, eventually I was published, and he paid me for my work.

Don't get it twisted. He might have been worth millions off and on and certainly when he retired, but he was as humble as they come. His upbringing in the South Side of Chicago was simple. As it was told to me.

1) "Don't snitch" (Don't want my baby girl in a ditch.)
2) ALWAYS BE HONEST, lies never end! Amen!
3) Be kind, nice is for fake people
4) Everybody is somebody.
5) Look everyone in the eye when you are speaking to them and Brooklin smile."
6) Lastly, no drugs, which will rob you of everything and you'll be stuck in timeouts in my office.

And that I was, but listening to demos" I loved it and found plenty of bands.

And since we don't lie, don't hang out with anyone so you don't have to. (I would listen to one part of that and months long stay in jail. He was so proud of me when I was released for not snitching and owning my piece in the puzzle.) The only time anyone is your business is when you are being kind. And always look everyone you meet in the eye.

"Oh, and Brooklin.

I'd begin to take my face out of my hands where it rested, my elbows leaning across his desk every time we had our talks. (Let's paint a clearer picture, if I didn't start carrying Aquaphor with me, my elbows wouldn't look younger than me.)

I would joke, "Daddy, my elbows need coasters."

And he would laugh and reply, "Right. What about work? Your time-outs are turning into quality time."

When he said that, it felt good. I was still realizing he was my dad, no matter what anyone said. He chose me, and those remarks would warm my less lonely soul. He taught me a great deal in the first thirty days I knew him, and he was still Dave to me. For a while, introducing me was awkward, as no one knew I existed. So, I waited for the day he introduced me as his daughter. The first time it was clear and not as a family discount, suddenly employees were holding doors open for me and security were greeting me differently. It went beyond me having a parking space and everyone knowing me in every other place.

Funny story. The only time I saw my ex-starstruck was one night outside the Roxy He said, "How are you getting us in?"

I started laughing. He hadn't met my dad yet. Nor did he have any clue what the last years of my life had been. I was smiling at security, already unhooking the red rope for me, and to accommodate his six-foot-ten frame. As usual, they lifted the rope up for me while the line went down the street past the Rainbow. I would slip through with Natalie, Danny, Courtney, "Him", Lethal Dose, (Erik is he felt like it) Hudson, and my oldest friends Spoon, Seth, Pep, and Boo Boo were usually across the way getting inked. Basically, we have been a crew since I'm a kid.

Dad took me next door once a week. Usually we'd go on Tuesdays. The place was notorious for its rock star history, which dad was a part of. He was also close with the owner, Mario. The Rainbow also had security who knew us and seated us in the second row of their famous, deep red, plush leather booths. We sat in the middle one. My dad was a regular way before me, and everyone knew. We ate the steaming authentic meatballs they brought us without ordering. We spent every dinner with someone who passed by purposely, and soon, I realized we weren't off the clock. Dad was still making deals without the ears of the corporate world.

Dad knew what was best, and it wasn't about taking money to make money. My dad firmly believes you have to give to receive. I was always naturally that way and realized it was one more trait that made me begin to believe in how right God was in his choices for my life—including the trials. The worst was done and told at the beginning of this autobiography of many lives lived and some died.

These moments were the kind I wished lasted forever. But Dad knew when to stay and when to go—whether it meant leaving Hudson with the thoughts Dad had left him with about his future or simply leaving leftover meatballs and a doggy bag we in the car. He was full of gifts, and it was no surprise. People knew my dad to be generous and kind. That was also why it was assumed I was his daughter before he proclaimed it loudly to Stevie one annual week before Christmas. We would keep the store open for celebrities to have privacy to look around, and Dad would always make more money by spoiling them. Give to receive and suddenly you are nominated for a Grammy or not, but choose to believe in yourself.

The night I began this memory, with my ex's jaw ending up on the ground, I may have not gotten that far. It's one of my favorite memories of him seeing me in my element. Being an NBA wife wasn't my thing. I was bored and wanted more. I found myself resentful at times. That was so even while I cried when he blocked Shaq and in less than fifteen seconds, his teammate caught his massive rebound with mere seconds left, pounding down the court with the hottest ball, dribbling for his life. Robinson stopped and made a career-changing basket from half-court—three seconds to the buzzer. I was crying with joy, knowing his childhood dream was to make the NBA, but really to block Shaq. He told few that, as people love to laugh at those who don't seem to belong. He was a white boy and a first-round draft pick who was a shooter, a power forward, and only now hailed for being ahead of his time.

The Hawks would make him a legend over a decade later, after many attributed the change in the game to his never-passed world record of seven fouls in a game and never taken out of the game. He also hit three-pointers and rebounds that game. He was valuable and, as a rookie, was put on the court a lot. I loved that feeling.

I still remember all the women who tried to get his attention, and he never stopped looking at me any chance he got. He even smiled when I would scream, "Bullshit," at a Ref. on a bad play—not exactly classy, but I knew how and when to be. First and foremost, it was my honesty and loyalty that he most loved me for. I will beat an idiot who wants to hurt anyone I love. He is more subtle.

Not that night in Hollywood, though. These NBA wife memories were already far behind me in 2003, as we had separated so I could move back to Hollywood and pursue my dreams. As you will find in this book, I had many aspirations and accomplished many, but fulfillment is a funny thing. I am learning it comes and goes. Or maybe I haven't found it yet? Having my children fulfills the biggest part of me, as did all those moments with my father and learning his gentle ways with others and me. On this same strip are where all these memories I'm rappin', rambling, and even scrambling all happened.

Before I tell you who made my ex's jaw drop more than the moment he knew he had made his childhood dream come true, I'll tell you that I've realized many times I had reached the top of a dream. I wish I had really sat in those moments. There were so many moments I rushed through. Like these run-on sentences my editor will hate me for, probably wondering what for too. You see these chapters are all different because my life changed constantly.

Before I knew it, it was Hudson, the best guitar player to my ex. yelling my name from the door. Yes, we have made it to the moment that unearthed so many memories. That's because Mr. Hudson was a common theme in my life since working with my dad—that and being posters on my siblings walls when I was only seven. I was searching for ChapStick as usual. I am unashamed to say I am addicted to creamy basic vaseline or Aquaphor products over the expensive shit people buy. More power to Revlon starting their famous line of started with lips products. Revlon Red turned into an entire line.

Funny how that is a perfect analogy of how my dad's unassuming career evolved. He went from being a drummer to managing the band he played in to managing others and dabbling in playing, before giving in to the corporate side of Hollywood. My ex. Husband's a bit more subtle than most meeting a childhood idol. Mostly through me, after having no clue until then, and the next day who my dad was and the realization of what my life had actually been without the knowledge of most of my east coast family for almost four years. I kept it from my ex. For almost two years. I was so used to not speaking on things. My ex. still doesn't get it. However, when you are told you can't even talk about when your whole life was violated and changed at ten. There is NO safe place. Except for my dad and also my first love, the budding rockstar, who were close as well. We're both there for me.

That night made me laugh and made me happy for my ex. from a small town. I thought I was being humble by surprising him. Seeing it is believing it to most. He is now using it against me as dishonest. This is why I kept my larger than life, life to myself. People would rather not believe it. They rather stay in their bubble. I looked up and saw Hudson coming toward us, his lips were moving, and I was trying to eloquently tell him to pick his jaw up.

My ex. never saw me that way. In fact, looking back at this very vivid memory, I see it was a moment of validation after he doubted his "fame" would get us into the biggest rock night every Monday for years. Monday night madness was a place only few got in. When I say few, I mean the chosen few. Once we went past the red rope, jolly as usual walking with us, my ex. gained composure quickly. But all night, he was wondering, *How did she do it?* "Roxy" was full to the brim. It could hold a thousand or more, but nobody waiting outside would be getting in. I felt bad at first. They had probably driven by and soon some commotion and wanted to see celebrities, and that was a no-no. I won't be telling you everything that you would see at every epic exclusive night, every single night of the week from Weho to past Hollywood and Highland.

Mondays were filled by two important spots, Joseph's with Bolthouse. Then on the other side of Hollywood, by 11:00 p.m., you wanted to be at the Roxy and in the crowd of music elite. Joseph's was the actors and producers, young and old, of Hollywood. Hugh Heffner would make an appearance every month with his blond posse. By midnight, they would be gone too. I skipped between them too, usually closing shop at the spot, the studio.

However, when my ex was visiting, I was less out there. His visits were for our heartbreaking hand-off of our baby girl. By now, she was two. This would go down until she was three—when three addictions got a hold of me. The first was Hollywood itself, not so much Hollywood, though I loved the excitement once I was closer to my dreams, my cousin (an actress), and my dad. The scene was my job, especially if it was scouting new bands, prospects to report back to dad. Many began to figure out I was working in the music business and wasn't just a Hollywood kid. I came out of nowhere at fifteen but never waited in one line. When you go out with a certain crew, the security and the promoters remember you and let you walk through from then on.

We had a job to do though—bringing in more musicians and producers. You know, it's like today's Instagram and those with a blue check and those who make sure to do anything but stay basic. I have been so basic while writing you all these memories that it may bore the fuck out of you.

My eyes are on fire and my brain too, and I want to cut off the waterfalls as they get closer to the dam that my memories, without a doubt, could burst open.

If I told you what I saw to my left and right of every memory, you would be like whoa, and I would be sued. So, I'm not writing about how everyone everywhere has a name you would know today. It was a safe place. And it was exclusive solely for the purpose of ensuring that no prying eyes who would ever be a source to the press swamped outside.

My friendship with Leo started with him having me grab his car from the valet and drive it to the back of the club, then "tacos" then home, as we found we lived close. We ended up spending 2:00 a.m. at Canter's deli regularly for the next year on random weekdays. That first time was one of Bolthouse's favorite nights while it lasted. Concord was a night for hip-hop. I was so tiny and using Mystic Tan daily, just to look alive not myself in less than two years this time.

All these moments mesh together because the thing about Hollywood is it barely changes. Faces and places do over time but not what is happening and the reason we misfits are where we are. Some are there to be pretty. Some, like me, are both to be pretty and to work for someone and for some reason or to protect those who they were working with in PR. If it was time to go to the studio, rounding up rock stars became impossible. So Lethal Dose gave me a key to get the spot ready. I'd turn it up and make it sing before everyone got there. Then we were shut in right before dawn. And if Le was in the mood, we would forget the time—unless I had my daughter off hours. His expression was obviously saying, "He is wanted here"

I don't know why he wasn't really wanted there anymore. I missed a lot in two years I guess. I assume dating someone I worked with and the rumors?

This is where I am going to stop the flood of memories because, as fast as these moments I grabbed, not just memories to me. They are the past.

Even my favorite memories. Like me and dad steaming meatballs on Tuesday nights at The rainbow bar and grill. We split all our meals. Now he wasn't making sure I tagged along. He was embarrassed. I sat in time-out, with him holding my phone for less than two days before I disappeared and spent the next half a year or slightly less away.

It went fast. I ruined everything I had achieved. My agency dropped me after my third movie fell through. I loved my job at Lethal Dose's studio. He fired me, until I went to rehab. I lost friends who were using more than me and would later be in the press. I have to believe I was saved from even more humiliation. The worst was when I went to "him" for solace. He let me in through his arm, which was propped stiffly on the door—almost like it was like an iron gate he was opening, not the front door I'd walked through more times than I could or should have to count. His head was cocked so far to one side it was practically on his shoulder. He was not stoked to see me. He was worried and tired. He didn't want to be associated with what I had become.

CHAPTER 82

Hollywood, like Love, Can Be Fickle

Hollywood is fickle, especially love. All those I love yous were floating out of every crack in that house we had shared—so much so he still claims my vivid memories weren't as deep to him. Whatever you say.

Then why, over two decades later, are we kissing by my aunt's window and those lemons that make me so happy in the Hills? We started our affair over twenty years earlier in these same Hills.

I resented my ex and still do for taking me away. Every time he took my daughter, he took a part of me I had to fill. I resented the abortion I kept from "him" and the baby kept from me. I resent that I was so nervous as he held me—still, after all these years later, the same. He tried. He did. I knew this was my last chance.

We FaceTimed my dad after hours in bed talking and everything passion does. I wasn't myself. I had made a choice to try to freeze my feelings, and it made me too much, and that's enough of that mistake. I knew my last chance to show "him" the real me again was now. A whole eight hours on a Saturday he gave me after he was openly fearful I'd be too much of something. I knew he wouldn't understand. He was more concerned with me not changing and still being the beautiful girl, I mean woman. He would correct himself out loud or with his eyes gazing into mine. I felt misplaced, and my confidence floated away like his memories of loving me. He kept asking me to move home. Those have floated away too.

The last day I saw "him," he walked faster than me to the car. (unusual) But I followed, He barely hugged me goodbye, which wasn't us. That morning we were so happy. Now at dusk, almost 5:00 p.m., he regretted telling me something. We were kissing, and I couldn't look him in the eye, ashamed of my inability to keep my emotions in check. What did I do?

Mere hours ago, he couldn't stop touching me for over a day and staring at me with desire and love. He said, "You have changed, babe." Then corrected himself, "in the best way." We laughed. Kissed and talked for hours about all the years we missed. Now things were falling apart, simply because of something he told me and didn't owe me. Yet I forgot everything my dad had taught me. I was twenty-four again, losing everything. God, not him. I was closing the dam on "him."

That last day has plagued me. I wanted to be transparent, and my healing is still ongoing. We go through all this trauma, and for most of what I have I would go through it all again, because I help so many. Why "he" keeps coming up is because I still have pieces to my puzzle missing. I am not completely free. He is the only reason I wish I didn't need the acceptance I get from my ex, my dad, my sister, and a few close friends. Many come and go in life, and this one has me puzzled more than absolutely anyone. I have lost plenty of friends for being a writer, for winning Maxim, for having a loving ex-husband who still treats me like his wife. If I crave coffee and mention it like that, within seconds of him getting home or my text, I have coffee or tea or a gluten-free grilled cheese next to me. I don't ask. It his love language. With my other two relationships, it was mine too. I have all this time to rewrite some of the same shit you already read.

If you are like someone, don't want respect. You will be accused of overanalyzing everything. It apparently isn't attractive. And I am sure you wish I had stopped at the lemons, or the steaming meatballs or Hudson being a moment I finally had because I was still successful and respected. I lost it all, and even him. For what? Everything changes. That vision is not the same if your anymore.

Thigh Highs and No Lies

He was the last thing left from my young wild years, and he still makes me feel free. I was holding on to him for many reasons. Maybe it was all inside my head.

And the car we laughed and kissed each other to breathe.
We're traditional and made it home to bed.
Sassy fucker, it's all vague now? Or will he.
Tik tok tik Tok
Where will I be tomorrow?
The rage is not the voice to listen to.
No one is a victim.
Choices
Not missing the moment you think where,
Check in.
It's human
Feelings are fickle.
Change the moment with positivity.
Never just hello or goodbye.
Your words
Hooked isn't it, vanity is lame.
Spill the sauce, dude, make a mess.
Burn my pizza
Whatever, I have to make some difference.
Not for my ego
And Jesus is everyone's memory
I believe what I see and to to rythme what we both
Perceived.
To the two Inover the most.
Forgive me for always loving you regardless.
The life we lived was different.
Then I ran far.
I know you both have changed and fuck I haven't
Taken a peak, I wish I could forget moments that
Made us different.
The right since those teenage days
Your truth wasn't about you or me.
It was not ithree ice cubes and laughing outloud.

Clown.

The talk blue you taught so much.

To this day I hear your care at times and frustrations as my disease got worse and my fate and yours was slipping away. I was the Angel in white you thought you would make you laugh forever and get better. I wasn't in time and suck it was the line What last forever? What returns and why? Who choose to peak in the life you made fresh and here we go, looking up I see you found me.

Smiling without a care, I offer you a screw and

Wonder are we all lefty Lucy's in this town wandering back because there is something.

A moment that is worth the ticking not one woo here living in digital. Sometimes alone and others with my son. Hopefully a familiar lover will be the break a woman, not a needy girl needs, but wants.

Needs are... Turning to you, fuck man you have all the screws and U have no ice cubes.

We'll never be perfect, but maybe a walk in the dark us astray, yo, don't make me laugh, forget I am Brooklin and can you not look at me with so much expectation.

Fresh hair and he may say now what?

You came and conquered the first part.

How it feels makes nonsense.

If it is what it should be it feels different, real,

And one day just Homies surround by static

No secret messages, that monster in you never scared me. The bitch in me is free.

This song came on as finished the last part.

What do it mean.

Love heals and it isnt a certain kind, but usually from the same innocent part of us that knows tonight is a moment and freedom is what we all deserve.

Stop the stop the judgment

The anger isn't toward her at all

Forgiveness isn't an easy pattern for most

For me, it's all I have to move forward and know

No time was wasted.

Not on that screw you handed me and a real moment changed that past. That shit fills one up really fast.
All that hate turns passionate.
Then if you could either not worry how long
Or when you can leave and make that
The reason why you don't bring that warmth
To the lonely girl who moved home finally.
You asked and zubaoways would, I had to meet
My shit straight, be courageous and know life is give and take and I Won't waste another day in hate it being hated for a bad day.
U have much to learn.
Not so little anymore.
But laughing over nothing
And then something switches the energy and
That thing that start the decades of passion
Reignites Don't worry about where this goes.
Far from lost, I have to make this work or I won't
Have all I want and daddy taught me.
Don't be mad if you remember me again.
Or if you text it don't.
Love your life.
Everyone wants to be the one he wants to make laugh more or that his kids recognize as a kind mother if her.
But we never had time to get out a decade of hotels and me feeling pressured for time. I'm home.
Dove soap and king wavy hair.
Botox is not my juice
Shut your mouth.
Still the youngest in the old crew.
What became of a lover tripped the electricity last time. Causing the divide. Unturned of the freak in me after weeks of you not wanting to be no good for me. Who says I want anything but a break. His name won't be told, but his story is bold and brave. He may hate me or see the truth. It doesn't take every day if our lives and the mistakes and other lovers or nights that unfold have and would have been.
I can't leave you out of our first kiss we didn't get to replace.

Don't lose your kindness, over your mind. There's no drama. I was being given life. I told no one who my dad was when I was auditioning, dancing, and touring. "He" may have been the first to know, as I ended up being at the office daily and became an assistant of sorts.

Fame is a faucet. My dad worked hard. Why did he teach me work? Dad made sure I worked for what I wanted, so I accomplished it. Before I would go anywhere, he reminded me not to say who I was, so I would earn it on my own. No problem—it made me work harder. Today, I am so grateful, and I was then, too. He made me work hard. My dad's name and notoriety grew massively over my twenty years in and out of Hollywood. Every time I came back, he had done something else unreal. What a great example. I write this book because I have him in me. This is such hard work, which is what Daddy loves.

Whether I was dancing on tours or had a child who would eventually wreck his office, he was proud. He went from one assistant and me bringing him coffee to five assistants. Then after I had my third baby, he had nine assistants. But I brought the coffee, and we went and had lunch. Otherwise, I listened and learned and went to studios to keep up over the years. I feel most at home in studios.

Soon, I was learning what brands of equipment to send to which studios and how. What I loved most was watching others' dreams come true. Music gets many through their worst days. I knew Dad was special, but it took me a while to grasp that he chose me. He tells me daily that I am perfect. It's so amazing. But also, as someone who has struggled with low self-esteem, I find it hard to grasp.

One of my favorite memories, out of many, was Christmas Eve at the store. Daddy would open the store for many celebrities—Sting, Slash, Eric, Yoko, and Sean; the list goes on. However, my favorite Christmas Eve opening was with "Stevie". We kept GC open late for him. Now, twenty years later, I have a blind / seeing impaired daughter. It really was a perfect night. and I know how amazing her life will be. This Christmas Eve, we kept the store open after hours for "Stevie".

My dad's favorite story to tell, to this day, involves Stevie.

Thigh Highs and No Lies

Joking, my Dad said, "Take a *look* around Stevie."

They had been friends for twenty-five years by this 2002 Christmas. Stevie had a great sense of humor. He laughed and, tapping my shoulder, said, "Tell your dad to fuck off. I know my way around."

It was classic behavior for both of them—lol. He even convinced my dad to let him drive his Mercedes that night (well, in the empty parking lot; Dad is still always down for whatever).

I could write a book based on stories from the twenty years I spent primarily in the Sunset GC or CR. He spent forty-four year in that office. Maybe another time.

I saw the wildest shit.

CHAPTER
83

On Fleek

If you wanted Hollywood secrets, though, I know them all, this book will be news to some. It won't be as simple as blocking someone. All those moments in my head, hidden away on dusty shelves, have been taking up too much room. I was told by a close Hollywood insider regular. (Yes, many in my life), "It's time. I know you. Every other thought is writing that book! More than we can count have told you for decades you should write a book."

OK, OK. Where do I start? Since then, the last time we talked, she has just been seen on the red carpet. I still see her as family, but life got away, and I hear it daily. "You look so much like her." I try not to laugh. Only my closest friends and exes know about Ang and me in LA. My life, for the better part of 1999 through 2005, was dancing on tours or working in the studio. Finding proof from the late '90s and early 2000s hasn't been easy. Fred is as kind as he was when he was my boss and friend. Because of my addiction, I lost touch.

Four years into my sobriety, as well as, my daughter's cancer fight, and this book brought some of the old crew into my life.

My Polaroid albums from tours, movie sets, and days in Heath's basement while he tuned all his guitars meticulously were stolen. We could be in his house for days and say a handful of words or have an all-night, intellectually driven dialogue. We hated politics, but unlike most, he wanted to talk about life, what we'd experienced, and how it changed us. He was the first friend I told about my rape. The memories of filming and friendships in a town that saved my life kept my mind busy. My adrenaline was always pumping back then from something (hope even).

The most unbearable part of every happy time was the background of my mother. She always had subtle threats under her breath out of nowhere. She always worried I would ruin her life by telling the truth. Ruin her life? I would go about my life. I was obedient until I couldn't be anymore—now.

Anytime I got away, even filming a movie or music video, something she'd wanted me to do when I was little, she'd say the same thing. "Whatever, you won't follow through. You fuck everything up." (She thought it scared me, each time she'd say, "You do know, no one out there gives a shit about you.")

A few times, I would hand the phone to my dad, after she had been heard on speaker. If she'd only known she was on speaker, she wouldn't have been so cruel to her daughter. I still would call until my late thirties, hoping this time she would be different.

I began touring as a dancer at seventeen. I'd had no guardians since I was fifteen. That tour would change my life. So did knowing I had a dad who was kind and sweet and truly loved and believed in me. When he took me to the Grammys, I became aware of his accomplishments, but that never changed how I looked at him. It was my life by then. From age seventeen to the time I was twenty-five years old, life was a whirlwind.

CHAPTER 84

Do You See a Junkie or Do You See Me?

I am me, and I was a junkie—once—but no longer the same. I have all my teeth, and my skin is clear. I'm not in debt, and I have a roof over my head. I shot heroin for the better part of eight years. I remember one of the last times I shot up. My ex was there. Don't hate him. He didn't want me to die. He held the belt and watched me shoot up. He'd never done that before. He watched my eyes roll back while I was still plunging the heroin-filled, bloody needle into my frail arm. I mumbled, "Let go." Then I sighed and said something he will never forget. "I love heroin." I crawled into his lap.

Maybe that was why he allowed me to use it. I showed love. I remember how high I got, knowing it was my last time. By this point, my ex. had put cameras in every room, so he could check on me all day. He was afraid I would die. My children never saw me use it. Nor did I have people over who used dope. I was very conscious of not allowing my children to see. Doesn't make it ok. Especially since I am well aware and should have known how much kids really do okie. It pains me greatly.

How does one start shooting up? For me, it wasn't a progression like most. I had taken pills earlier in my twenties. Then one night at my successful and now close friend's house where he used openly. I became curious as a group of very successful players in Hollywood were partaking. If they could, so could I, rig. I am sure I looked interested before I finally asked for some. He was very free-spirited and kind. He shared, and I assuredly said, "That way," meaning the needle. I shot up for the first time, no questions asked.

For the next year I would only use with someone who could shoot me up or I wouldn't use at all. Eventually, I became like a nurse when it came to finding my veins. Many get addicted to the ritual. Maybe I did too. Heath didn't like being alone. He brought me to the set of *10 Things I Hate About You*. I became one of the "girls on the bleachers." Heath said, "Come to the set, sit." And he sang. I ended up in the background and on the cutting room floor.

Another good friend, Tashina, was in the party scenes. Heathie and I were listening to records in the Bohemian basement of his otherwise medieval-style house in the "Echo area." He was rarely there, working always. I stayed with his best friend, and house-sat for him a few times. He called me a lovable, trustworthy, trainwreck. Nice, I laughed.

Within five short years after turning 20:

I went from high-end Hollywood and money to jail cells and even a homeless shelter for almost a month. And then there were the rehab stays. I was completely numb by this point.

I used heroin for a long time because I got away with it. It makes me sick now to think how the world works. Even when the law did catch up with me, I had my bag full of dope, and I'd just put a needle in my arm, while driving. When I was pulled over, I broke it in half and shoved it in three different places. I knew the searches. I remember one of the girls I was arrested with saying, "You take it and shove it somewhere. They will make you cough three times." I looked at her dark eyes, which matched her beautiful chocolate skin tone, my own eyes glossed over, no longer bright. I was so high, yet I remember this clearly. I said, "OK," almost immediately.

The last time I saw her, I was being released, and she was being booked. My body was still full of hidden drugs and paraphernalia. No one even knew I had a life in Hollywood. Yet, ironically it was my name on the street—Brooklin in Hollywood. Everyone knew me. I had worked hard, before I finally fell apart. That evening she was still being searched as I was being freed, without enough evidence to keep me. There was plenty. It was all over me. I had all the dope on me. Was it because I didn't pick my face or look like your regular scar-faced, trigger-happy junkie? Oh, I've had my moments.

On the set of *"Hustle"*, I let my career get taken away by lies. Someone planted drugs on me and had me framed in the makeup trailer years before I ever used. Why didn't I fight? That began my spiral. The night before I lost my job, I was hanging out with some friends, and I rejected the lead. That scarred me to this day. I hadn't even done drugs much then. Within months, my broken heart finally gave in. Until then, I'd used my pain and brokenness to accomplish things most don't achieve.

I want to add, since my daughter's cancer, I have lost a great deal of motivation. I walked an hour a day and spent up to ninety minutes practicing yoga. Then my daughter got sick. My days were consumed with hospitals, and my nights, with fear and tears. Here we are, almost three years cancer free, and now she is blind. I have still not gained my energy back completely. Fight or flight is exhausting. I am just grateful I didn't relapse over almost losing my child. I was traumatized.

Do you get triggered?

This book isn't about blaming. Nor is it about many in my family. This is about overcoming trauma and most of us have dissociated ourselves from those who didn't protect, believe in, or care for us and, worse, disappeared. I was blessed to have a family given to me. My dad (Dave Weiderman) is a gift from God. My mom doesn't try.

This isn't a game. This is real life.

Aside from a bullshit holiday, I stay away from toxicity to this day. Some force themselves and feel awful afterward. It used to hurt to feel alone. So did her manipulating love language. I speak the truth. People don't like that so much sometimes.

It's sad because when I gave in to the filthy truth about myself, that's when I began to find myself. I became self-aware *and realized* I'd better fucking care about more than myself or constantly fleeing from emotional realities.

CHAPTER 85

Sour Cream and Polar Bears

Who the fuck brings sour cream to the best party on earth? That would be my roof top with "Del taco" talking about saving polar bears way before climate change was a topic. My friend of years had won an Oscar for dying because of these icebergs he wanted to save for the polar bears. I couldn't help but look at my taco and realize most of my real conversations had been over them. There were staples to real family? Good friendships, and real connections equal family. After I'd moved to Hollywood at fifteen, most of my friends were Mexican American. I was grateful to learn the meaning of family.

Finally and thankfully, family meant something to somebody. It never meant more to them than anyone I ever met, even traveling the world. The Spanish, Germans, and Italians showed me what *familia* really is. Yet, I still sit and wonder, *What have we Americans done wrong?* In barely two hundred years, we have fucked it all up again and again.

I remember sitting at a table, wiping my mouth after eating perfect tamales Spoon's family—

Yet, I clearly remember thinking history isn't safe with us. What have we Americans done? I began to understand the divide.

Today, twenty-four years later, my oldest daughter is in college studying political science. The reason? Simple. Like me, she is sick of the division in this country—what the United States calls freedom. My daughter has given me more courage to write this book than anyone. She'll tell you to your face, every which way to Sunday. Are we fucked? Depends. Let's listen to the kids and what they're saying. Do you want a future? They hold it.

In other words, "America the Great" doesn't matter; it's nothing. What's your first thought? I ask anyone who is reading my wild mind on this paper in perfect lines. Maybe your mind is firing without a direct shot. Or like me, do you immediately think of your family? Or also like me, do you hide from the inevitable? (Hypocrisy on fleek.) Shit, we're only human, as they say. But, my friends, we are the only ones who can fix it. Forget about the end or what it's supposed to look like. Try not to worry yourself about the polar bears, like I do. Try to find a way to survive. We're also animals. We're human, and survival is a daily necessity, a device, a bomb ready to go off. So let's unarm ourselves.

Questions?

This book is about you and me. It's about life as it is and will be. I'd love your feedback.

CHAPTER 86

The One Who Stays— and Gets Away

My friends. As you know, it goes deeper, and it's valid. At one point, you had love from someone, and time muddles things. The industry does so, especially with love. Being in love with a man who can have anyone because of what they do has never bothered me. I knew them. All three men I have loved have been famous at every level. I was cool with all of them until recently. My ex is my biggest supporter and has accepted my heart for "him" and, lack, thereof of marriage. He knew about my pregnancies and how young I was to go through so much.

They were both aware that I had abuse in my childhood. However, not until I was in my late twenties and early thirties did I flat out tell them, "I was raped at ten."

"His" reaction, at first, was silence as he looked out the window of my high-rise. Silently, he looked into the distance, and silence is something we can be together. But I became afraid I'd scared him. Great, Brooke, more baggage and shit. So I downplayed it and said, "Never mind. It was forever ago. I didn't tell you for some reason." I remember feeling stupid and my bare body standing in the middle of the small living room, gold light coming through the tiny windows. I moved just my body to the side to grab the T-shirt to cover myself.

It turned out he didn't walk away from me or what I'd said. He was composing himself, because now, he was a father of a daughter.

He said, "Don't cover yourself or apologize. It's taking all of me not to hurt him and your mother for not helping you since you first told me pieces over two decades ago. I wish I knew the whole story before. Though he gathered. He said straight faced "Brooklin It explains the running and the neediness phases." I went in and out of being not there and too there. We both did and didn't know why?

(Many were hormonal or drug related, but I am sure I clung to him most because he was the first man I was with after what I would figure out was a fuck, later to be confronted with "Brooklin you were raped." I was thirty three when I really heard it. But I knew. Just never said the word. Why is the word so taboo still? The act is still so viable in society, and real.

My first experience of what lovemaking, fucking, sex, and kissing was supposed to be.) He taught me everything I knew. I wasn't ever nervous with him, and I needed him to know that.

I feel like he backed off most after my transparency. I had begun speaking publicly, working at child advocacy, and had been asked to write a book for the first time twelve years ago. I shared it with him in anticipation he would find out publicly. Also, don't assume "him" is all "him."

He told me a few months ago, "I never want to hurt you or be a jerk. But, man, you know how you get to me more than anyone." He went on to say, "I used to think you were needy and texted back too quickly. Then I thought about how much you leave and how I have no idea where you will be next."

I cut him off and said, "Basically, we're the same person, aren't we?"

He started to agree and then stood up and said, "I don't know, Brooklin. Can we just be us?"

I jumped up in my black lace panties and lacy black tank—my style since we met and now all he ever wanted me to wear.

Over the course of these decades, we had both been in relationships with others. Then we'd found our way back to each other somehow, but I think that is over.

Life is a trip, for sure, and "he" has been one of my longest and shortest all at once.

CHAPTER 87

Music to My Eyes Every Time

Like me and my dad, he was always in the studio and part of one of the most popular white rap groups in the '90s. He went on tour with Beastie Boys and every rapper you can think of. He was on some of the Family Values tours. Some artists, like Ice Cube and other acts, were special guests, rather than part of the original set list.

To "rap" this up, I fell in love and again was in a rock star relationship. However, D took me out publicly. We went to Dragonfly on Sunday and Joseph's on Monday together for over a year. We worked together, and soon he was living with me, and his ex was stalking me. We took my Escalade and sat under his balcony with my friend Spoon while she threw his shit over the side. As long as he got his customized hop guns, his platinum records, his new lyrics, and his art supplies, he was good. That was a crazy day.

So was that relationship. I sabotaged it, too, with dope. He hated me high, but I tried. That's when I began sneaking up the hill to see "him." We had run into each other at a celebrity wedding party and spent weeks together. My daughter was being picked up by her dad the day after we packed up what "he" wanted me to wear—that same lace. All those feelings came back and fast. I had muted him for the past two years. I had been in Hollywood, less than five minutes down the hill from him, and hadn't attempted to see him.

I saw him at Ivar on a tiny street in the middle of Hollywood. It was the first band I found at my dad's office release party. I was leaving, and we caught each other's eyes. Mine teared up, or maybe it was all the paparazzi? I ran to my car and sat in the driver's seat in a dark alley with two girlfriends who had no clue. James and Courtney are aware now and would be there for the next decade of whirlwinds. Then, they didn't know who he was to me, and until the way he looked at me, I had forgotten too. I went back and he grabbed me and put me on his back through the rain and the paparazzi. I tossed my keys to my girls and shrugged. They would soon figure out this wild ride I kept deep inside. We spent a week together, then I went back to my life. Our connection was still scary and life had changed so much. His fame had risen even more and yet I didn't care what people said. I knew what we had, even though he seems to forget apart.

It would be only weeks until Carmen's rehearsal dinner, where we were seated across from each other. Carmen whispered, "Put you with a hottie. It was the universe. And it was that night that would really set us back in motion—until my daughter's cancer and the pandemic eighteen years later would we really never be the same? But who is?

Exploitation this love said:

I was telling my daughter's heroic story. The one story she wanted to share of her overcoming Cancer beginning at a tender age of eight as exploitation. No it is her amazing strength and her story helping others. The same way I hope to. She is my mini-me and I am beyond proud of her. No matter what she does. He used to praise me for my strength in handling her cancer so well and apologized for not knowing how sick she really was. It didn't upset me that he wasn't there—until the moment I realized why.

I realized recently relationships are perceived so differently and some are fickle and change drastically. My being gone was a rejection or a choice. I had no choice. I never would have left. My choices and my own trauma drove me away. I had beautiful babies and, every time, would miss ours.

Thigh Highs and No Lies

To all of you who have a similar story and still wonder why, like I do, I'm sharing with you openly, I never planned to. But I allow spirit to guide me when I write. It drives me nuts, as this book is supposed to be in print by now.

Food for thought—since this book got publishers and I have done a cover of a Magazine *at 41* and other opportunities, I have lost many.

When you are low or high, you will see who is there and who isn't. That's OK.

Time does heal, but don't wait for anyone too long. When someone wants you; misses you; and, fuck, respects you as a human, they would never let hateful words be the last lyrics hanging from the hook.

But really it's about coping with the past. I used to believe I should be judged. I fucked up my life. I didn't. I allowed pain to go deeper and deeper, until my tummy always hurt or the lump in my throat felt like it might burst. Instead of talking about my childhood abuse, I used dope to numb what had been done to me.

Friends, please talk about it, even if those closest to you don't believe you or choose to ignore your situation. Those closest to me, indeed, knew what happened. We have resources now. I'm writing this book for anyone who relates and wants to accomplish their dreams but finds that pain keeps them from moving forward. Pain does that; it causes us many symptoms, all leading to the same place—feeling alone, fearful, or fearless if you need noise. Please stop thinking everyone knows, even feeling crazy. You are magic. You are strong. You are loved. And you have a whole world waiting for you.

Remember this: There is a place for everyone at the table.

CHAPTER 88

Don't Touch the Lemon Tree

It would be sixteen more years, and more drama would unfold. While I was put away at another place that was supposed to fix me, my dad resigned, Weinstein finally got caught, and Spacey disappeared—except he was where I was the whole time.

I was at the WW house; Yeah, it was supposedly confidential. However, just like me, it was leaked on national television where some of us were. I was merely a civilian in comparison. All the same, we ended up at the same place. Supposedly, it was a place that was exclusive to the stars? What stars? I could tell you, but I don't feel like getting sued. I do know everything that happens in that incest pool of a town. So many wish they were in the crowd or even the rearview. No, you don't. That will just haunt you.

They got inside my mind and I finally made this book happen. I had left many of my stories off my bookshelf my whole life until my thirties. It is common to remember later in life. It's how we survive.

Question for anyone reading my story?

Do you relate? What do you relate to? We all have something similar and it is time we focus on that. That is a part of equality's fight. Finding the similarities in our stories, no matter where we come from.

I just keep thinking, What in bloody hell made me so fucking easy to take advantage of, like a duckling, but not the ugly one? I had an advantage. I knew. It's disgusting, but it's the truth. Then that world, especially in Hollywood, like much of my grammar, is full of run-on sentences.

    Reality is a bitch. And think of the abuse that happened during that time. I am so sorry. I was terrified daily for those hearts without faces haunting me—alone since who knows how long but now with nowhere to go. Breathe.

CHAPTER 89

Child Move Forward

Facts—writing this has made me dizzy, similar to getting off a roller-coaster ride.

I know no one wants to really know there's a dark force. But there is. It's real.

You *are* already loved and worthy. However, turning loss into power and rising above the pain is where you become you. Release the fear and all the demons who hold you. You and your experiences that caused so much pain are real. That's why I'm writing this—whether in the rain or on sunny days in Cali, my happy place, inside instead of enjoying the warm Februarys. I missed so much.

I am back home in Hollywood to be inspired—to be able to focus.

It feels infantile at times, I know. The battle for souls isn't about perfection or shallowness. That doesn't come close to what we wear or swear by. But what you think and what you say can save lives.

Chapter 90

No Bullshit!

Tell your story friends.

Use your voices, your heart has a story we can all learn from, a talent we all need. Jokes we all need to laugh at. My hairstylist is seriously an artist. We all have something others can't live without. Don't look down on others. We are just here trying to work this thing called life out. When someone is in your life and on your mind, reach out. There is always a reason. Don't give into what others say, remember who you are together. Nothing alse matters, than what only you are able to transfer with a clean heart to another.

Rip to the fearful souls that will soon be exhaling without fear or an anxiety pill. Interact. Ask for help. I hope to hear from you and know you are OK. You're so courageous.

I hope you know you aren't alone. Nothing is as it seems. We all have our own mindsets, mouths to feed, payments we have to pay. We push forward. That's what keeps us going. I think of my life in Hollywood and my loves, career, and friendships. I was passing red ropes, no idea how, but it's what it was or who I was married to or worked with or looked like. I didn't care. I made beautiful friends along the way, many of them cheering me on as I write this book.

As I sat down to type another day, I breathed heavily, ready to focus on this book again, for you. There is so much I am going to tell, and much of what I say may leave you with questions. Hopefully, we will meet, and I will, without fail and with complete vulnerability, answer how, when, or why. The next chapter should help you understand the undeniable truth. This is my first book. It's formed from my worst pain and memory, which ultimately shook me to the core yet also shaped me into many forms over the years.

Then becomes her—with this amazing life all everyone sees. But I remember going back to school the next month. My birthday was just weeks away. I also swore everyone knew something had happened to me—that I looked different, that I was different.

One boy in sixth grade said, "You are quieter than you used to be. Are you OK?"

I just nodded and looked away, so I wouldn't cry.

It was the first time anyone had shown concern. Yet, he had no clue what for? He helped me feel seen again, in sixth-grade math of all places. I used to be the class clown. It would take a few years to find my silliness again, but the wild child was on the prowl by twelve. In seventh grade, the anger came out. These would be the first years my mom would finally consider me being able to meet my dad, because she couldn't handle me. Looking at me, her guilt had to be eating away at her, right?

As a mother now, I could never imagine not running over (accidentally, of course) the person who hurt a child, mine or yours. Especially someone who'd hurt a child in one of the vilest, if not the vilest ways.

How could she expect me to have boundaries, when she'd shown none the night her daughter's life was flipped upside down and she did nothing. Writing this book, I told myself I would be truthful, vulnerable, and try not to point fingers and blame bad experiences for my later (poor) choices. I still made the choices. I knew right from wrong. We all do. It's in our gut. You feel it when you cross that line. It makes me sick.

My dad would teach me mostly about four main character choices—to be truthful, to love music, to not snitch, and that all you need is love. He would save my life—and not just once. Spiritually, he was sent to me, for me to believe in myself again and to have hope.

Pay attention in your lives. There are some who go and some who stay. Never make anyone stay or take those who stay for granted.

The universe wants it that way. I was never taught the birds and the bees or anything past that. No elbows on table, and napkins in your lap. In other words, look good, and all will be OK. Don't think about it, and it will all go away.

Facts—it only gets worse. Walking through the trauma and going through it are both courageous, but they're not the same. It's a process. Are you ready to walk through the pain to get to the other side?

It's OK to be completely unaware if it wasn't your fault or if it was the new bikini you had just bought and worn. Let me tell you, *No, it was never your fault.*

It's not, and I mean both. It wasn't your fault or the bikini. You did nothing wrong. Whether you were touched, neglected, forced to do things you didn't want to, or raped, it's not your fault. Losing someone you love and so many other experiences cause the same receptors to go off. Trauma is trauma. There is no comparing the effects or the pain. Your story is your own, and it left you broken, as well as (for most of us) feeling alone and trying to piece it all together.

How can we? Trauma is devastating regardless, and no one can tell you how to feel or not feel at all. And oh they will.

Chapter 91

Cancer, not Candy, Ya Ass, Trauma not Tan Lines

My daughter has had more lollipops than I could ever count, making her nickname Lolipop. She was eight when she got sick. I was in Hollywood working on a streaming show. My career was taking off again. Then I had a dream of my daughter, who I would visit every six weeks, along with my other children. I didn't have my youngest son yet. I did get pregnant with a boy soon after my daughter's diagnosis, I was no longer with my Son's Father anymore, however his coming gave us hope. However, before that, my dream about my daughter had me on a red-eye plane that night. I felt in my God gut and my mom's gut something was wrong. I never thought it would be a brain tumor, though. I still have guilt to this day. Would you ever assume a brain tumor with headaches and blurry vision? We thought she needed glasses. My mother swore she was dyslexic, which was ridiculous, and we ignored the suggestion. My relationship with my mom is absolutely sad. I have worked hard for the good moments, but all in all, she resents me for the life I have been given. Yet, she forgot what I overcame. My daughter, with her brain tumor, was about to overcome her own trauma. We had no idea of the trauma our eight-year-old was about to endure. Her biological father wasn't able to deal. That is all I will say about him regarding this, because she had my ex, who raised all the kids as his.

Once we realized one eye had lost all sight, we were shocked, she had an MRI in days. She was admitted that night and spent the next six weeks in and out of the hospital. She had her first of three brain surgeries the third day she was admitted. She handled it like a superhero. I was a mess, of course—at first. Then I roared. I never knew how strong I was until I watched my baby girl overcome trauma around the same age I'd had to. I had no support, and no one believed me. It is still traumatic, and her fierceness is a huge part of why this book had to be written—because you are not alone.

My daughter ended up having five rounds of chemo and lost all her hair. We never cried so hard as the night her hair fell out. It was a Symbol, we had lost control and Mommy couldn't fix it.

She is cancer free today. However, cancer did take her eyesight. I won't go into depth, as this is her story to tell, and she gets upset. She is a beast and reminded me of all the children suffering from trauma and feeling alone like I did.

My daughter is now well. At almost a handful of years cancer free, she remains mostly blind from her cancer. Which she handles with more courage than I knew anyone had. The cards we are dealt become our story.

What will I ever know compared to her? One thing is true, we moms are beasts—untamed when it comes to our babies safety, but aware. We're ready to pounce if you even look sideways at our kids

Unlike when my worst trauma was happening, I held my child and cried with her. I cradled her all night and the next day, until she was ready to cut it all off.

However, my rape wasn't treated with any feeling or compassion at all by those who knew.

This has stuck to me like glue, though; to me, it's a good analogy. Then like my daughter's hair, it fell off everyone else like it wasn't real. It still does to this day. I didn't tell anyone until I was older, out of fear and embarrassment. And mainly I didn't talk about it because, who would ever believe me, when my own mother walked in and told me, "It's not that bad"?

Today, more than eight years since I told my ex-husband, he knows the reality, and I know it's hard to process. But worse, it is happening every minute of every day still, around the world. It's happening in your neighborhoods, in glass houses.

I was encouraged to share her story by her. Even when she gave me her blessing, and I sent her cute messages to the world and other sick kids just minutes before her first of three brain surgeries, my comments section was still a mixed bag of dicks and dames. People are unbelievable.

I'm experienced in therapy and therapeutic ways to heal. As well as digging into how people react and respond, to trauma, patterns, and their ability or inability to deal. People find this difficult, even when it isn't their own life. On a post like mine, a mother and her strong and yes sick child are sharing, and you willingly choose to leave a nasty comment. Sad really, get a grip, trust me every life has improvement, and everyday.

Painful, but the cruelty was so obviously sick. If ever wondered why people don't share their traumas and pain. So many people will downplay it or, worse, completely throw it in your face like trash.

I knew the whole time. If my child was going to have a tumor, if she is going blind from it, can we get to the point and kill this tumor before it kills my daughter. I was ready to fight.

I felt like I did at ten. But this time, this was my eight-year-old baby girl. I had to snap out of it and remind myself I wasn't a child. And though I wasn't making it about me, seeing my daughter at almost the same age about to face trauma hit me hard. My daughter handled everything so well. I wouldn't leave her side—not until they made me. For three weeks, I never left her side. The first day home and recently finding out I was pregnant, I just threw up and cried and slept for sixteen hours straight. I realized I barely slept for three weeks. I just stared at my baby, not knowing what her sweet baby heart was saying every moment.

She wasn't naive anymore. By week three, she had changed. Slight depression had set in. She was healed from her second brain surgery. The chemo had begun, and she llost her hair within ten days.

My baby asked me a question I will never forget. "Mommy, if Jesus is kind and I love him, why is this happening to me?"

After all my healing throughout the years, I finally had an answer that had saved my life when I allowed my trauma to break free. I was thirty-three, then my daughter was almost nine. I told my daughter the only truth I know, and that is this is the devil's world, not ours. These bad things that happen are not Jesus. He heals us or brings us to heaven. After a long life a lot of healing and one home. (Heaven)

We cried because I began begging Jesus not to take her, and a peace came over me. She is a warrior. She is you, and this book had to be written after these past three years watching my daughter's completely different trauma than my own trigger many of the same behaviors. We had many of the same traits after the pain—anger, depression, bad dreams, needing constant reassurance.

Thank God, I was willing to fight without the support of anyone after my trauma. My daughter is a fighter, and she me, her Momma right here. I was a beast and fought for my daughter. Doctors were wanting to give her more rounds of chemo, after her blood was cancer free. I said, "Jesus, you saved her, and I am trusting you Lord, not from humans.

My distrust brought me so much faith and took away my trust in mankind. Do we have to choose?

Not just believe. Like me making the choice.

Not letting my daughter go through more rounds of poison." Does it help later? Do they remember you fought for them? Sadly no.

But Mommas, Advocate for your children. Believe their pain. Never doubt them, no matter what. Regardless of how crazy it may sound, never leave your children feeling alone. Trust them. The truth always comes out, and it isn't about you or what you believe. It's about believing in your babies, that is our job.

How am I different from my mom? I am only human, as cliché as that sounds, but I am a beast for my babes.

Without a beat, I'll tell you, I hope, dream, and always smile at complete strangers. No gain intended, but love spread. I hold and console my babies.

CHAPTER 92

Bullies Are Made at Home

All moms should have biker boots to wear for a good ole' PTA meeting or to confront the jerk parents with bullies for kids.

In my trench to cover my pasties and tank, I walked straight to the principal's office. Yes, they were all aware I was coming. I made the principal laugh about something off topic as I waited for the parent I would be confronting today. When my daughter lost her hair to cancer, it becomes a weekly occurrence for a few months of me having to show myself directly—which makes "Zen" mom's ear blow smoke. Yes, you can do yoga or pretend to and raise a cruel creature at the same time. Sad really. Like I've said, "Glass houses."

In this case, the mother had received over twenty-two notices, and her second-grade daughter was almost expelled. She still refused to hear that her daughter was not just hurting feelings; she was behaving cruelly. Unfortunately, bullies are made at home. How the mother could have nothing kind to say after my daughter was bullied for losing her hair from chemo was beyond me (still is). I had already felt badly for this child. Who was full name is strong and full of such virtues. Does Eli know that her full name carries a great many accomplishments?

Moms, shit, women want to be liked, even if they find you annoying. So always look for cues. For instance, this day, I was dealing with the mother—However, we were here because a friend of my child's called in tears at the horror of hearing my daughter being called names—in other words, because of her daughter's absolutely horrid behavior. Her daughter had told the whole school, "My daughter is ugly, contagious, and dying." Instead of immediately summoning her daughter for such behavior, the mother scolded me for categorizing her child as a bully. You said it, not me. So the war of a mama bear was on.

We have to set boundaries and teach our kids to do so early. I was sticking up for my daughter so she could see how it was done. It was the last time she ever needed me to set anyone straight—with assertive kindness and acceptance. You don't like me, cool. Then keep my name out of your mouth, please.

That day, the principal knew I was coming and all the write-ups this bullying child had against many kids, including mine. I won't apologize for doing something about it.

It became obvious why kids are who they are. You aren't helping your children by excusing their nasty behavior to save your name. Trust me, everyone is looking at you both sideways.

Though when you read this it may not seem like I took a breath, I had done that, along with taking off my trench coat and getting comfortable. The other mother, on the other hand, couldn't look up or stop rolling her eyes. Humility is as important as kindness.

This is true even if you or anyone you know is being bullied.
Bullyville.com
Bullying is serious.
Dedicated to my youngest baby girl.

CHAPTER 93

Charmed (They Say)

Years kept passing. My life looked charmed from the outside. I was lucky, true. I promise you, none of that matters—not if you feel like you're living a lie. I couldn't hide from myself. Life always moves on, from the outside.

As I type, my toddler son is sprawled across me, watching some YouTube learning show. He's so relaxed, without any worries, with his own iPad at almost three. I know. What's the world come to? All the while, my TV is also blaring a Netflix crime drama in the background. Forensics has always interested me. Still, obsessively, I type this story, my story. As I place each puzzle piece where it belongs. Hopefully painting the picture clearly and as honestly as I have asked ahold everyday to guide me. Many people won't like what they don't know, never knew, or wonder why I never spoke of so many things. Because I was told not to and the reactions Ibhavebalrwady received from people I thought were actual friends. Think about your own life. Who really knows everything? No one, but you and those who shared the moments I chose to share in this book.

I worked meticulously, feeling guilty every time I had to stop, even to be a mum—Was I guilty I wasn't fully there. Maybe, but we have to make sacrifices to create the life we want those we love to have. I want my kids to be unafraid, to know the truths of life. It isn't all rainbows. But there are plenty waiting.

Thigh Highs and No Lies

Life never stops, not for anyone, and it certainly won't because I'm writing a book. Have I mentioned that enough? Am I trying to convince myself that I'm finally doing this? I'm filling blank pages with the full ones in my head. What's the hardest part for me? Putting each piece of me where it belongs. (the word itself belongs)

We have to learn a few things in life and it being ok not to belong or even want to if someone won't let us be ourselves is what leads us to our authentic selves. Not staying and trying to belong. Fuck that!

Belongs? Where does anything belong? Of course, there's a timeline—and an exact one. However, when you spend most of your life suspended between one experience to the next, separating what you remember clearly, in full scenes, it's tricky to want to be honest and remind myself, this isn't to blame anyone. This is to bring awareness, peace of mind to anyone struggling, freedom to myself and hopefully to anyone feeling caged. Not knowing no your worth is your worst enemy.

Then there's the fact that time brings fear to many, whether or not it's an inevitable part of life, aging.

Immediately, I go back to tapping my foot and staring at the clock until the bell rings—like I'm sixteen again. Early or late? Time can be a daily cage we have to work ourselves in and out of.

Emotional contortionists, does anyone never feel trapped in themselves? Or do we all feel caged? Then freedom should bring relief, right?

For me, like most things, I felt disappointment, even rage. In the end, I was never free at all. Even once I finally accepted what had happened and knew deep inside it wasn't a death sentence, I still lived half alive most of my life. Honestly, I wonder if anyone could tell. I was living to make others laugh and falling in love young and too fast. Those and other behaviors directly related to a broken heart. I am grateful for my capacity to love, my heart stayed beating with hope.

I chose not to be the walking dead over and over again. We will fall, it is never the fall, it's not getting back up. We're beautiful vampires, afraid of nothing and everything at the same time. Sunlight blinds and then kills the pain you lived with all your life.

I loved.

CHAPTER 94

Presently

I'm sprawled on my nice, expensive bed. Twenty years later, it's all still replaying. Here I am, putting it all on the line. I'm using my voice and what stripped me of so many things, so much so, I'll actually never know. I have daydreamed of who I might have been if I wasn't raped and then left alone in pain—a ten-year-old with no prior knowledge or understanding of what had happened to me. I was devastated, yet I didn't know why. I wept silently, until I was completely dry and dead inside. I fell asleep holding my knees and woke up biting my tongue. I always thought, *How symbolic*. I would be doing that for the next thirty years—until I couldn't bear it. I couldn't bear the thought of anyone becoming a shell of themselves.

Liberation isn't too late.

We are working toward liberation. Many other cultures won't even touch others or wear certain colors.

Some even shower up to five times a day.

Maybe that is where we Americans have gone so wrong.

Why is sex so casual?

And of course, it's traumatizing in other ways.

This is why one of our largest epidemics is derived from sexual deviance. Love is beautiful, and so is sex. However, one without the other isn't the same thing. Something is always missing.

CHAPTER 95

If It Makes You Miserable

We are all paying a price by sitting here being miserable, not doing what we're put here to do. Your gut is your compass, friends.

Listen to it, or it will only get louder.

When we don't listen, we drown in it with other distractions from our purpose. No judgment. I still struggle. Hit me up on my websites and use the resources I wish I had. You aren't invisible.

Lord, if I don't bring this down for a landing, finishing this book, my whole mission and moral compass will be off forever. To be fully present, we have to pursue greatness. To me, that's freedom. The universe will bring you to the end if you start. It's in your gut, you know what you are meant to do. It isn't impossible. You are here and it is only you who is given those cards that have become your story. It's uncomfortable, not going to lie.

Staying comfortable the last facade has been worse for sure. I know I have for too long. Or we say fuck it, say so long to the old and on to the better version of what is already in us.

Can I get an amen to the God gut who told me to tell you? I get sick too. I fuck up, and I get tired. I am one bad choice away from throwing it all away. Whatever your poison, you are your own cure. For me, this book is one of mine.

CHAPTER 96

Clichés

Truly, I thought turning forty was the end.
But, really after all, I'm still here.
It's a new beginning. I won't say it's the new thirty, but it is new.
We all wear masks some days.
Life seems kind some days and cruel others. However, we keep going.
A new beginning every day or just start, just today?
Until next time.
I have much more to tell you—about hopes and the time Jesus told me some awesome shit that kept me going instead of letting go. Don't let go. Nothing is easy, but everything is worth it. Until next time, friends.
Remember, wake up to *live, not to resist.*
I want to get rid of everything I inherited from her—*my* mother. Yet, forgive, I want to forgive her and find peace for her also.

Brooklin

CPSIA information can be obtained
at www.ICGtesting.com
Printed in the USA
JSHW021913290623
43956JS00001B/38

9 798889 821724